THE PERFECT GENEROSITY OF PRINCE VESSANTARA

Frontispiece. Vessantara talking to his wife and children on Crooked Mountain; Vessantara gives his children to Jūjaka. Mural. Mädavala Raja Maha Vihāra, Kandy District. 1755.

The Perfect Generosity of Prince Vessantara

A BUDDHIST EPIC

Translated from the Pali and illustrated by unpublished paintings from Sinhalese temples

MARGARET CONE
AND
RICHARD F. GOMBRICH

OXFORD
AT THE CLARENDON PRESS
1977

Oxford University Press, Walton Street, Oxford OX2 6DP

OXFORD LONDON GLASGOW NEW YORK
TORONTO MELBOURNE WELLINGTON CAPE TOWN
IBADAN NAIROBI DAR ES SALAAM LUSAKA ADDIS ABABA
KUALA LUMPUR SINGAPORE JAKARTA HONG KONG TOKYO
DELHI BOMBAY CALCUTTA MADRAS KARACHI

British Library Cataloguing in Publication Data

The perfect generosity of Prince Vessantara:
a Buddhist epic
Bibl.
ISBN 0-19-826530-1
1. Title 2. Cone, Margaret 3. Gombrich, Richard Francis
294.3'3'3 BQ5815
Mythology, Buddhist

Printed in Great Britain
at the University Press, Oxford
by Vivian Ridler
Printer to the University

PREFATORY NOTE

THIS book is intended both for the general reader and for the specialist. The general reader is invited to read the Introduction, perhaps skipping section II, and the translation; he is warned that the story of Vessantara proper begins only in the middle of p. 8.

The *Vessantara Jātaka* has been translated into English only once before, by W. H. D. Rouse in 1907. That version is neither accurate nor attractive; we have been unable to profit by it in preparing our own.

Our illustrations too are entirely new; they are photographs taken by Gombrich on a visit to Ceylon in 1969–70. Text and illustrations are intended to enhance each other, for we hope that by showing how one Buddhist society has pictured the story to itself we have added a dimension to our readers' understanding of what Vessantara means to ordinary Buddhists.

The two Appendices are intended to serve the interest of the close student. Appendix I is our translation of what the text labels 'The Long Description of the Forest'. This tedious botanical catalogue, inserted before the story's climax, may well have built up suspense in an audience already familiar with the plot, but can only dishearten the solitary reader; moreover, it would defy the literary aspirations of any translator, even if he could be certain exactly what trees and shrubs are meant. Appendix II notes all the points at which we have deviated from Fausböll's printed text (often at the suggestion of Professor Alsdorf), as well as mentioning the few places in the text which we consider hopelessly corrupt. Our purpose in it is merely to show what we have translated; we have not re-edited the text.

The numbers in the margin of the translation refer to the pages of Fausböll's edition of the text. For the note [*Cp.*] see p. xxx.

The authors have divided their labour as follows: Margaret Cone has made the translation (including Appendix I), incorporating a few suggestions from her co-author; Richard Gombrich has done the rest.

ACKNOWLEDGEMENTS

THE illustrations have been made possible by great generosity. The photographs could only be taken because of the selfless enthusiasm of Mr. P. A. G. Jayaratna, who worked any number of hours a day driving me carefully to remote places, holding flash guns, and providing valuable companionship. The use of the car and the loan of Mr. Jayaratna's services I owed to the munificence of Major (as he then was) A. A. de Alwis. On most journeys I was accompanied by Mr. Y. P. Jayatissa, who sacrificed all his spare time for several months to helping me in this and related projects; he and I shared equally the actual taking of the photographs, so that about half the illustrations in this book—it is impossible to say which—were taken by him. To such a friend I need make no further public acknowledgement. Mr. K. G. Dharmaratna and Mr. R. M. U. Dharmavardhana joined and contributed to some of our expeditions.

Back in England, most of the technical work on the illustrations was financed by the Oriental Faculty of Oxford University and ably executed by Mr. Martin Amor. Finally, the colour plates would not have been financially feasible without a grant from the Astor Foundation; this is but one of the many benefits I owe to Sir Isaiah Berlin.

RICHARD GOMBRICH

CONTENTS

LIST OF PLATES

COLOUR PLATES

Frontispiece. Vessantara talking to his wife and children on Crooked Mountain; Vessantara gives his children to Jūjaka. Mural. Mädavala Raja Maha Vihāra, Kandy District. 1755.

MONOCHROME PLATES

Between pages 16–17

1. Painting on cave ceiling (plastered rock, uneven surface). Kaballālena Raja Maha Vihāra, Vällāgala, Kurunegala District. Late eighteenth century?
   (*a*) The Buddha calls the earth to witness his generosity.
   (*b*) Māra is defeated and tumbles from his elephant. The *L.* side of this photograph overlaps with the bottom *R.* of (*a*).

2. The birth of Vessantara. Mural. Toṭagamuva Raja Maha Vihāra, Galle District. 1805.

3. Vessantara is installed as viceroy. Degaldoruva (see Pl. C (*a*)).

4. Mural. Däḍigama Vihāra, Kegalle District. 1907.
   (*a*) Vessantara levitates, worshipped by his parents (apocryphal episode).
   (*b*) The marriage of Vessantara and Maddī. The two scenes are contiguous.

5. Hanguranketa—see C (*b*).
   (*a*) Vessantara at home with his family.
   (*b*) Vessantara gives away the elephant. The two scenes are contiguous.

6. (*a*) Vessantara gives away the elephant; on the *R.* is an alms-house. Mural. Käḷaṇiya Raja Maha Vihāra, Colombo District. 1888.
   (*b*) Vessantara gives away the elephant. Toṭagamuva (see 2).

7. (*a*) Vessantara gives away the elephant. Mural on plastered rock. Daṁbulla Raja Maha Vihāra, Matale District. Mid eighteenth century.
   (*b*) The brahmins take the elephant off to Kalinga. Mural. Baṁbaragala Raja Maha Vihāra, Vaḍuvāva, Kurunegala District. Early twentieth century?
   (*c*) The citizens complain to King Sañjaya. Same site as 7 (*b*).

8. *Top half*: Vessantara gives away the elephant. *Bottom half*: he gives away horses and carriage and, on the right, food. *Bottom R. corner*: Jūjaka is sent on his way by his wife. Painting on

cloth. Agrabodhi Vihāra, Dehipāgoḍa, Kandy District. Early twentieth century. Possibly by D. S. Muhandirama, who painted in the shrine at this temple.

the Cetans; he declines their offer of kingship, but takes his leave; they escort him to the edge of the forest. Consecutive scenes from Degaldoruva (see C (*a*)).

20. (*a*) Vessantara with the Cetans. Giddava (see D (*a*)).
(*b*) The Cetans see him off. Hanguranketa (see C (*b*)).

21. Details from Arattana cloth painting (see A). (*a*) and (*b*) go *R.* to *L.*
(*a*) Vessantara and family proceed after leaving the Cetans, and mountain spirits watch as they rest and feed the children.
(*b*) Someone points out the way to them (apocryphal episode: confusion with Accuta?); they are seen by the god Sakka.
(*c*) Maddī and the children in their own hut; they visit Vessantara in his; the almost obliterated figure in the air on the *R.* must be Vissakamma.

22. (*a*) Maddī with the children in her hut; Vessantara looks after them while she (the damaged figure on the far *L.*) gathers food. Kaňdulova (see B).
(*b*) After Vessantara has talked to his family, Maddī gathers food on Crooked Mountain (shown by the maze) and her hut stands empty. Mädavala (see Frontispiece). This scene adjoins the frontispiece on its *L.*
(*c*) Vessantara takes the children to his hut for the day. Degaldoruva (see C (*a*)).

23. (*a*) Amittatāpanā's parents cannot repay the money which Jūjaka deposited with them, so they give her to him in marriage, and he leads her off. Toṭagamuva (see 2).
(*b*) The women at the ford mock Amittatāpanā. Mural. Arattana Maha Vihāra (same temple as A). Second half nineteenth century?

24. (*a*) Amittatāpanā castigates Jūjaka, so he sets out to find slaves for her. Arattana cloth painting (see A).
(*b*) Jūjaka says goodbye to Amittatāpanā. Mural. Sapugaskanda Maha Vihāra, Colombo District. *c.* 1950.
(*c*) Same subject. Giddava (see D (*a*)).

Between pages 64–5

25. (*a*) *R. to L.*: Amittatāpanā at the well; she threatens Jūjaka; he says goodbye and sets off; he gets lost in the forest; the Cetan forester threatens to kill him; Jūjaka cajoles the forester. Käḷaṇiya (see 6 (*a*)).
(*b*) The Cetan threatens Jūjaka. Dehipāgoḍa (see 8).

INTRODUCTION

I

THE selfless generosity of Vessantara, who gave away everything, even his children and his wife, is the most famous story in the Buddhist world. It has been retold in every Buddhist language, in elegant literature and in popular poetry; it has been represented in the art of every Buddhist country; it has formed the theme of countless sermons, dramas, dances, and ceremonies. In the Theravāda Buddhist countries, Ceylon and South-East Asia, it is still learnt by every child; even the biography of the Buddha is not better known.

Here is the story in barest outline. Prince Vessantara, the son and heir of Sañjaya, King of the Sivis, and of Queen Phusatī, lives in the capital with his wife Maddī and their small son and daughter. His munificence is unique. He has a magic white elephant which ensures adequate rainfall, but he gives it away to brahmin emissaries from another kingdom. The citizens are enraged, and force Sañjaya to banish him. Maddī chooses to share his exile with the children. Before leaving he gives away all his possessions, making 'the gift of the seven hundreds'. After a long journey the family reach a mountain glen, where they settle down. A vile old brahmin called Jūjaka, harried at home by a young wife who demands servants, arrives to ask him for his children, and Vessantara gives them while Maddī is away gathering food. Next morning Sakka, the king of the gods, fears that Vessantara may yet give away his wife and be left all alone; he therefore disguises himself as a brahmin and asks her of Vessantara. On receiving her, he gives her back immediately. (As he now has her as a gift, Vessantara is no longer entitled by convention to dispose of her.) Jūjaka and the children come to Sañjaya's court, where Sañjaya ransoms his grandchildren and Jūjaka dies of overeating. Full of remorse, Sañjaya takes his retinue to the mountain and invites Vessantara and Maddī to return. The family is reunited, Vessantara becomes king, and all live happily ever after.

The Vessantara story translated in this book is the oldest surviving version, or at least that which contains the oldest surviving material; it is also the longest and fullest literary version known to us. It is in Pali, the ancient Indian language in which the scriptures of Theravāda Buddhism are preserved. It is called the *Vessantara Jātaka*, and is the last and longest story in the *Jātaka* book, which constitutes a part of the Pali Canon, the scripture of Theravāda Buddhism. A *jātaka* is a 'birth-story', a story of one of the former lives of the historical Buddha, Gotama Buddha. (Gotama is a family name, Buddha a religious title meaning 'awake', 'enlightened'.) Before his final birth Gotama lived countless lives in various states of existence in heaven and on earth; of these the *jātaka* collection deals with a mere sprinkling, conventionally said to number 550. (This is a round number: in fact the Pali text has 547 stories, and later collections have added various non-canonical stories which are supernumerary.) In all *jātaka* stories the future Buddha is born on earth as a man, a good spirit, or one of the higher animals; he is usually the hero of the story, but if there is no character suitable for identification with the Buddha he is a spirit who witnesses and comments upon the events described. In very many cases there is nothing specifically Buddhist about the story itself: its religious application is clearly secondary and indeed superficial. In fact the *Jātaka* book is one of the world's oldest and largest collections of folk tales.

Each story has a preface which describes the occasion in his preaching career which prompted the Buddha to tell it, and a brief conclusion in which the principal male character is identified with the Buddha and the other characters are identified with the Buddha's relations, disciples, and enemies. For instance, the male villain of a story is always identified with the schismatic monk Devadatta. In our story, Devadatta was the hideous and despicable old brahmin Jūjaka, who asked Vessantara for his children. For the key to our story see p. 96. By linking 'the present', i.e. Gotama's life, to the primeval past, the *jātaka* stories have for Buddhists the function of a charter which in a sense justifies actions and ordinances of the Buddha. Many of the stories originate in the *Vinaya Piṭaka*, the part of the Canon which lays down the rule for monks and nuns.

By now the informed reader may have raised an objection. Is it not true, he may ask, that Buddhist doctrine denies the existence of the soul? In that case, how can Vessantara *be* the future Buddha? It is perfectly correct that according to orthodox doctrine no *person* is reborn; when a man dies, his *karma*, his moral bank balance for good or ill, passes to another being who is conceived at that time—in heaven or in a good station on earth if the balance is good, in a mean earthly station or in hell if the balance is bad. The new being is neither the same as, nor entirely other than, the old. But in the context of myth, poetry, and story this subtle metaphysic is ignored, and the rebirth of a being is treated just as a simple-minded westerner would understand it. The doctrine is not *contradicted*, for from the religious point of view it is the moral continuity which is relevant, and over-simple expressions such as 'I was Vessantara' can be explained as 'conventional truth', a convenient shorthand; but to the average participant or listener the doctrine is in this context of no interest.

For in this series of lives the Buddhist sees a simple teleology: the Bodhisattva, the future Buddha (for that is what the term means), is preparing himself for his final life, in which he will rediscover the basic truths of existence, preach them to the world, and be freed from the cycle of rebirth, his mission accomplished. According to developed Buddhist theology—or rather Buddhology—which certainly postdates most of the stories, the Bodhisattva is throughout these lives developing to their highest pitch certain moral qualities which are prerequisites for Buddhahood; and according to Theravāda Buddhology these qualities number ten, and the first of them is 'giving' or 'generosity'. (The inelegant translation 'giving' correctly suggests that the quality is understood literally, not metaphorically.) There is another book of the Pali Canon, one of the last added to it, entitled the *Cariyā-piṭaka* or 'Book of Exploits'; it sets out to recount the lives in which the Bodhisattva attained the ten 'perfections'. The story of Vessantara, an example of the perfection of giving, is its longest chapter(see p. xxix below).

The story of the Bodhisattva's exploits as Vessantara has a particularly close connection to the story of the Buddha himself. In the preface to the whole *Jātaka* book it is related how the Bodhisattva's penultimate birth, the one between being Vessantara and being Siddhattha Gotama, was as a god in the Heaven of the Delighted. (According to a tradition which is not among the earliest, Siddhattha, which means 'having attained his goal', was Gotama's personal name; he discarded it on attaining Enlightenment.) Thereafter, when the appointed time had come, he descended at the invitation of the gods to be born from the womb of Mahāmāyā, wife of Suddhodana, who was king of the Sākya people within what is now Nepal. After a childhood spent in princely comfort, followed by disillusion and flight from home, he culminated six years of wandering and mortifying the flesh by enduring a particularly severe fast. When this failed to bring him the peace he was seeking, he again accepted cooked food, a bowl of milk-rice, and at dusk made a seat beneath a peepal tree, determined not to rise from there before he had attained Enlightenment. The account of his spiritual progress during that night is given by the texts in two forms, the literal (in terms of the truths he realized) and the figurative. Figuratively it is said that when Māra, the god of Death and Desire (which for Buddhists are two sides of one coin), saw that the Bodhisattva wanted to escape from his realm, he assailed him, riding on his elephant Mountain-girdle and accompanied by all his hosts. The good gods all fled in terror, and the Bodhisattva realized that he was left all alone, with no defence but his moral perfections. Māra rained on him nine kinds of deluge, all in vain, and then ordered him to leave his seat, claiming it as his own. The Bodhisattva refused to leave his seat, and with his ten perfections rendered Māra's weapons powerless, so that they rebounded. They then disputed who had the right to the seat, and Māra's army bore witness to his generosity.

Then Māra said to the Great Man, 'Siddhattha, who will bear witness to your generosity?' The Great Man replied, 'For your generosity you have sentient witnesses, but I have no sentient witness. Leave aside the gifts I have made in my other lives: in my life as Vessantara I made the great gift of the seven hundreds, and to that this solid earth, though

> not sentient, bears witness.' He took his right hand out from under his robe and extended it towards the great earth, saying, 'In my life as Vessantara I made the great gift of the seven hundreds—do you bear witness to that or not?' Then the great earth roared, 'I was your witness then,' as if scattering the forces of Māra with a hundred roars, a thousand roars, a hundred thousand roars. Then, as the Great Man concentrated on his gift as Vessantara, the elephant Mountain-girdle, who measured a hundred and fifty leagues, knelt before him, acknowledging, 'Siddhattha, you have given the great gift, the supreme gift.'

At this Māra and his hosts fled in all directions, and the gods sang a paean of victory. This version comes from the introduction to the *Jātaka* book.

The recollection of his generosity as Vessantara is what assures Siddhattha's victory over the forces of evil at the crucial moment and enables him—as we learn in the next few lines—to realize the Truth and obtain Enlightenment. His calling the earth to witness is one of the favourite subjects of Buddhist art; in Theravādin iconography (see Plate 1 (*a*)) the Bodhisattva, seated cross-legged, extends his right arm straight down in front of him, the hand vertical, palm outwards, while just in front of him a small female figure, the Earth personified, emerges from the ground, visible down to the waist; in front of him and to the sides, if it is a three-dimensional representation (e.g. a four-walled chapel), Māra and his army flee in confusion.

It surprises us that the particular act of generosity recalled is not Vessantara's gift of his family, which is the *raison d'être* of the story, but rather the gift of all his goods on the eve of his departure into exile, an event which plays a subsidiary part in the plot. Nor is the gift of the seven hundreds normally reckoned as even the second most important episode of the story: that place is held by the event which causes Vessantara's banishment, his initial gift of the magic rain-bringing elephant. Not only does this episode seem crucial for the plot; it is in fact the episode which artists depicting the *Vessantara Jātaka* illustrate more frequently than any but the gift of the children. In Sinhalese iconography, if the Vessantara story is to be shown in a single scene, it is Vessantara's gift of his children to Jūjaka that is almost invariably chosen; just occasionally, as at Daṁbulla (see Plate 7 (*a*)), the single scene portrayed is the donation of the elephant. For the Bodhisattva's choice of the gift of the seven hundreds as his highest boast to Māra we can offer no conclusive explanation, but suggest this: that Vessantara inevitably sprang to mind as the paragon of generosity because of his gift of his children; and yet this very gift occasioned in Buddhist minds qualms which would mar the mood of the passage. The gift of the elephant, on the other hand, owes its importance to the plot of the Vessantara story and cannot be so well generalized as the straightforward gift of all one's material possessions. So this latter gift is the one with which to trump Māra in a simple contest of generosity.

Having earlier referred to Vessantara's gift of his family, we have narrowed our reference to his crucial gift by calling it the gift of his children. The gift of his wife Maddī forms a separate episode which follows the gift of the children, and, being Vessantara's final act of renunciation, it might have been expected to constitute a climax; but the reader will soon find that the episode is in fact rather an anticlimax, and extremely brief compared to the central episode with the children. Moreover, in most of the Sinhalese temple murals which we have studied the giving of Maddī is of minor importance, so that it is sometimes even omitted. Postponing for the moment a comment on the lower cultural value of the wife, we may make an observation on the structure of the story. The giving of the children has pathetic possibilities which are exploited to the full: the children lament as they are led away, an episode which is even duplicated by allowing them to escape; and Maddī can lament the whole night long as she searches for them. Vessantara may lament only briefly, because he must show fortitude, just as Maddī must when she finds out that he has given the children away voluntarily, and again when she herself is given. Thus the opportunities for lamentation all cluster round the giving of the children; those opportunities are taken; and the episode becomes the story's centre of gravity, lengthy and heart-rending. But Indian stories never have tragic endings, and Vessantara is to get the children back in the end, so his fortunes must start to mend, that the happy ending may not be too abrupt. From the literary standpoint it is therefore appropriate that his gift of Maddī should be the turning-point. It is the turning-point for Vessantara because it is in a sense a pseudo-gift: although Vessantara does not know it, we the audience know that the aged brahmin recipient is the king of gods in disguise, and is about to give Maddī back to him. In fact he gets back in reverse order everything he has given—including even, in other versions than ours (see p. xl), the miraculous rain-bringing elephant. So the gift of Maddī is the emotional turning-point for the audience, a calamity which will instantly be remedied, and not a moment of great tension.

But more is involved than the formal literary consideration. For we are in a world where it is the man's unquestioned right to dispose of his family as he thinks fit. Such rigid patriarchy was more typical of ancient India than it is of modern Ceylon or South-East Asia, where women traditionally have considerable rights; but even in these contemporary cultures, male dominance is sufficiently assumed for the Vessantara story to be emotionally credible. Marriages were of course arranged—not that this precluded love and affection, but many men were no doubt more interested in their children, and particularly in the continuation of their line through sons, than in their wives. It is worth remarking, for instance, that in ancient India before the Christian era sons inherited all, and in the absence of sons the widow was not even a residual legatee. (See the passage on p. 29 on the bitterness of widowhood.) Moreover a man's funeral rites after his death were performed by his sons, not his widow; Buddhists discountenanced the old brahminical belief that only surviving sons could save a man from hell, but to this day it is the sons who play the leading part in Buddhist funerary rites.

In theory half of the average audience at the preaching of the *Vessantara Jātaka*, or at the recitation of a poem based upon it, could be women; but in practice, we suspect, women formed the great majority of most audiences. Whether any male auditors would identify with Vessantara is doubtful, for he is too apparently superhuman; but certainly the women could empathize with Maddī. The loss of a child is in poor countries an experience all too familiar. Maddī's lament must be the passage in the whole work to which the women would most readily respond.

Parents in Buddhist countries do not lose their children by death alone. Many of them go so far as to give away their sons, not indeed to slavery, but to a monastery; for this is held to be a layman's supreme act of piety. In the monastery the sons are likely to be comparatively well cared for materially, but the parents lose their emotional relationship with them, and in many cases physical proximity as well. Moreover, the loss of a son is a heavy economic blow in an agricultural community, or indeed in any community where sons are the only security in old age. The renunciation of one's child—though in this case it does not occur against his will—is an extreme case, but not a rare one, of the difficult experience, which almost all Buddhists undergo, of exchanging the goods of this life for spiritual benefit, for 'merit'. Some anthropologists estimate that in modern Burma villagers spend a quarter of their income on religious donations (Spiro, 459), and that one in every ten males is a monk (Spiro, 284), besides which almost every Buddhist male has an expensive religious initiation (followed by a brief novitiate) before he becomes fully adult (Spiro, 234–47). Admittedly this intensity of religious activity is the highest observed in a modern Buddhist society; but it may well preserve the moral climate of pre-modern times.

Maddī and the children may arouse empathy in the audience, but they are not moral agents. The moral problem is that of Vessantara himself: is it right to give away one's family? We may cite the parallel of Abraham and Isaac; but to quote a parallel is not a moral argument, and besides, the Buddhist theological position is far from the Hebrew, for the question of obedience to a supernatural power hardly arises. Buddhist ethics require a word of explanation here. They are an uncompromising ethic of intention: the morality of an act lies not at all in its effect but solely in the intention, the thought behind it. Thus it is no good giving something away if you regret it, as Vessantara himself says (p. 63). The point for the Buddhist lies not in the nature of Vessantara's gifts, but in his becoming so free from attachment that he does not mind parting with anything. Of that detachment his gift of his family is only the culminating demonstration. It is certainly not that he wants to be rid of them: for the Buddhist, dislike is just as great an evil as attachment, for both are manifestations, positive or negative, of desire. Enlightenment is attainable only by freedom from all desire whatsoever. (Unfortunately this point is somewhat obscured by the redactor of our version of the story; for he ascribes to Vessantara a desire for omniscience, which is a late technical term for Enlightenment. Even a craving for Enlightenment is a craving, and thus an obstacle to attaining it; but a moment's reflection will show that it is the last craving which has to be abandoned. Obstacles such as attachment to material goods and family ties are necessarily encountered earlier on the path to perfection.)

When this has been said, the view that it is selfish to hand over one's family into slavery for, or as a sign of, one's own spiritual advancement still remains, among Buddhists as well as among Western readers. In Ceylon we found Buddhist monks to opine that Vessantara had acted wrongly. Further inquiry would probably encounter more such feelings, mixed with notions of the inscrutability of the ethics of such superior beings—rather like the reactions one would expect from Christians polled on their feelings about the story of Job. Preoccupation with one's own Enlightenment to the exclusion of concern for others was of course the accusation levelled against the older schools of Buddhism by the new school, Mahāyāna, which developed around the beginning of the Christian era. Mahāyāna Buddhists held that a true Bodhisattva would not attain Enlightenment, and thus achieve release from rebirth, before he had brought all other beings to the same salvation; that is one reason why they gave less emphasis to the historical Buddha. In our text too there is a trace of the same idea: when his children run and hide, so that he cannot present them to the brahmin, Vessantara calls to them: 'Come, my dear son (/daughter), fulfil my Perfection. Consecrate my heart; do what I say. Be a steady boat to carry me on the sea of becoming. I shall cross to the further shore of birth, and make the world with its gods cross also.' (p. 58.) Scholars have argued that this sentiment is no part of the original story; be that as it may, it is in the text which has been current in Theravāda countries for about two thousand years. That text thus contains an implicit hint that

Vessantara is doing something dubious for the sake of a greater good—ends are invoked to justify means.

Moral unease about the gift may have reinforced the obloquy which our story heaps on the brahmins. After all, Vessantara would never have given his children away if he had not been asked for them. And who but a brahmin would make a request so vile? Moreover, brahmins make all the trouble by asking Vessantara for the state elephant in the first place. Logically, the request could have come from any emissaries, but brahmins it had to be, because our text is an exemplar of Buddhist anti-brahminical sentiment.

Buddhism grew up in the late sixth century B.C. as a protest against Brahminism—though of course it was many other things as well. Brahminism, the dominant religion of the time, was a sacrificial system monopolized by hereditary priests, brahmins, who had to be paid for their performance of domestic and public rites. They claimed unique social status, and generally held that the road to heaven, at least for non-brahmins, lay in paying sufficient sacrificial fees. Liberality was praised, but principally if brahmins were the recipients. Although many brahmins were not priests, or were priests only part-time, economically they were mostly parasitic on the richer farmers and on the merchants who at this period were emerging as a new middle class. Several new religions arose to challenge the brahminical monopoly. Buddhism, not in all ways the most radical but ultimately the most successful, was distinguished by its ethical emphasis—and its ethic was an ethic of intention. The moral quality of an act depended not on its effect but on the intention behind it. Thus, Buddhism did not deny the caste system, which was simply a fact of the social environment, but stripped it of religious significance: the true man was the inner man, the true brahmin the wise and holy man who lived in truth and self-restraint. Brahmins were attacked for performing sacrifices (especially animal sacrifices) and satirized for their greed. Jūjaka is the apotheosis of the satirized brahmin. At first, in his marital troubles and his hardships on the journey, he supplies an element of farce. But ultimately he is a bogyman pure and simple—as the children point out. Without his despicable request Vessantara could not have reached the peak of self-sacrifice; but the bad man gets no credit for occasioning virtue, and Jūjaka goes straight to hell.

Buddhism abolished religious donations to brahmins, and declared that purity of mind was all; but it did not abolish religious giving. A serious Buddhist was—and is—supposed to become a monk or nun, renouncing material possessions and family ties—almost like Vessantara. Buddhist monks replaced brahmins as an economically parasitic class; they are wholly, not just partially, dependent on lay charity. Although doctrine stated that the sentiment accompanying a gift was of paramount importance, this was somewhat compromised by the concept of the suitable recipient: in a kind of litany which most Theravāda Buddhists learn and frequently recite, the Order of monks is called 'the supreme field of merit', which means that it is better to give to them than to anyone else. Similarly, in the Pali list of 'the Ten Good Deeds' which became popular in medieval Theravāda Buddhism, giving is the first; just as giving heads the older list of the moral perfections to be attained by a Bodhisattva. The importance of giving is probably the favourite theme of Buddhist sermons; and the giving envisaged is the religious donation. In fact the Pali word for giving, *dāna*, which is used in all these contexts, has come in Sinhalese to mean a meal given to a monk or monks!

In real life one cannot have one's cake and eat it: what is given is gone. Only in myth and fantasy can one have it both ways. Vessantara gets back everything he has given away. He gets the spiritual reward for renunciation; but his forfeit of temporal advantages proves short-lived, and in the end he becomes king and even wealthier than he was at the beginning. His reward is both on earth and in heaven; and the supreme reward of Buddhahood is still to come.

We are now in a position to conjecture why the story of Vessantara holds its unique position in Buddhist countries. It is not enough to point out that it is a fine story, full of pathos and dignity—though certainly it is interesting that another story of a man who gave away his family, Hariścandra, is extremely popular in Hindu

Bengal. We posit that a story, like any other social phenomenon, is most likely to survive and flourish when it answers the most disparate purposes, in other words when its appeal is overdetermined.

Culture in Buddhist countries is traditionally dominated by the clergy; they are the arbiters of taste. We talk here of the Theravādin countries, where Buddhism is dominant in large areas of fairly homogeneous population; the same may well be true of Tibetan Buddhism and the parts of Nepal and Mongolia over which it extended. In the villages of these cultures, the only public art which is not ephemeral is likely to be the art of the monastery temple; and what shall be depicted there is determined by the monks. The temple is not only the centre of ritual; most Buddhist ritual involves sermons, and sermons shade over into story-telling, and, in some countries, into drama. Finally, all traditional education was imparted by monks, and the monasteries were the centres of literacy. Thus it is monks who dominate the cultural scene and choose its themes; and however much the *Vessantara Jātaka* may appeal to the laity—and we have suggested that it appeals especially to women—we must ask above all why it should appeal to monks.

We have already suggested an answer. The *overt* message of the *Vessantara Jātaka* is the paramount importance of giving—the first of the ten perfections, the virtue which defeated the god of Death and Desire, the monk's favourite theme. This giving, however terrible, is shown to gain every kind of reward. But the story has for the monk also a *covert* appeal: like him, Vessantara has renounced all worldly ties, and in particular all family ties; and though the moment of separation is painful, such renunciation has its own appeal. We are not referring primarily to the public commendation; that certainly exists, but for most family men it would be inadequate compensation for their loss. We are following rather a bold suggestion put forward by Professor Spiro in his study of contemporary Burmese Buddhism: that the institution of Buddhist monachism answers to certain regressive character traits; that it can serve as a charter for narcissism, in that a monk has no social responsibilities whatever. Vessantara's first chance to get rid of his family is thwarted when his heroic wife rejects his suggestion that she take another husband and insists on accompanying him to the forest; subconsciously, giving them away is a consummation of that impulse. The monk's self-centredness is the object of ambivalence, both for the laity and for himself; but the weight of Theravādin culture is behind him: to shed responsibilities is to do no wrong.

II

A short essay on the development and diffusion of the *Vessantara Jātaka* may here be in place.

We have mentioned that the Pali version here translated is the oldest one surviving. From this Pali version are directly derived the many versions in Sinhalese, Burmese, Thai, Cambodian, and other South-East Asian languages. From it or from something like it, moreover, derive all the other versions, in Sanskrit and Chinese, in Tibetan and other languages of central Asia, the versions current among Buddhists of schools other than the Theravāda, and even among non-Buddhists. In essence, then, it is the original of which all other versions are translations, paraphrases, or re-creations—in essence, because the Pali text which has reached us is the final product of a long period of oral transmission.

Our text, like the other Pali *jātaka* stories, contains both prose and verse. The verses were memorized and handed down, accompanied by the substance but not the letter of the prose passages connecting them. That there were such prose passages in all the *jātaka*s is clear; though the verse includes narrative, the story is never fully intelligible without interspersed explanations. At an early date, Buddhist exegetes declared the verses of these texts canonical, so that to vary them was not permitted; the prose passages, on the other hand, are with very few exceptions to this day not canonical, but rank as commentary, which imparts to them a lesser sanctity.

Jātaka verse bears unmistakably the marks of oral literature. It is full of stock phrases and epithets, even when these seem not to suit the context: both Prince Vessantara and his magic rain-bringing elephant have the epithet *Sivīnaṃ raṭṭhavaddhano*, 'bringer of increase to the kingdom of the Sivis', and Vessantara keeps it even when he gives the elephant away to foreigners. Tellingly, these epithets occur most frequently at the end of the line, where the metre is most rigidly fixed. Elsewhere the metre is free, and so is the grammar; both contain archaisms, and both are, by classical standards, occasionally incorrect. Sometimes the verse is corrupt. For these reasons, its meaning is not always clear, and was never felt to be so; occasionally even the ancient author of the prose passages seems to have misunderstood it.

These remarks on the oral character of *Jātaka* verse apply to our text to a peculiar degree. Perhaps because of its length, the *Vessantara Jātaka* has the character of a folk epic, unique in Pali literature. Stylistically, it is in places more closely comparable to the great Sanskrit epic, the *Mahābhārata*, than to anything in Pali. There are long set pieces in which couplets are repeated with the variation of just one word; these we assume were songs. Moreover, the resemblance to the *Mahābhārata* is based on acquaintance: the long catalogue of the local flora and fauna is closely modelled on a passage in the *Mahābhārata*.[1] Although Professor Alsdorf (see next paragraph) thinks that this passage was inserted by the original author to heighten the suspense before the fateful meeting of Vessantara and Jūjaka, and although we agree that in oral recitation it may have such an effect (whether or not an 'original author' intended it), we have relegated it to Appendix I, because it is unreadable in translation. As for the ways in which the author of the prose has misunderstood the verse, generating new features and episodes in the story, we shall return to these below.

The only modern study of the *Vessantara Jātaka* which has any value is a long and learned article by Professor Alsdorf,[2] to which we are much indebted. Though unable, for reasons which the first part of this Introduction should make clear, to accept his conclusion that the kernel of the text, consisting of the old verses, is 'completely un-Buddhist', we accept his stratification of the text and most of his emendations (listed in our Appendix II). Alsdorf[3]

[1] The latter part of *Mbh.* III. 155 in the critical edition (vol. iv, Poona, 1942).

[2] See the Bibliography, p. 110.

[3] In his dating and linguistic examination of the verses Alsdorf is, as he says, largely following Lüders.

shows that the verses are extremely old—he even contends pre-Buddhist, which would mean before 500 B.C. He detects in them traces of translation from other dialects, notably from Magadhi Prakrit, spoken in north-eastern India, the area in which the Buddha himself lived. This harmonizes with his conclusion on other grounds that the story is originally set in that part of India, and that the mountains to which Vessantara is banished are not the Himalayas but are in what is now called Orissa. (So the title of Maddī's song (pp. 19–20), 'Description of the Himālayas', is a misnomer.) Further, Alsdorf detects some dialectal peculiarities in the verses of the prologue in heaven. This prologue, as he points out, is but tenuously connected with the main story. His conjecture is that it serves to link Vessantara to the lineage of King Sivi (Sanskrit: Śibi), famed in Indian legend for giving away his eyes to a blind man and other immoderate acts of generosity. Alsdorf even suggests that the *Vessantara Jātaka* formed part of a cycle of legends connected with King Sivi and his line.

Alsdorf points out that according to the prose the first verse of the *Vessantara Jātaka* is that which Fausböll's text numbers 20; the story is well under way, and Vessantara is about to give away his magic elephant. If we set aside the prologue in heaven, this is indeed where the old verses start. The other verses which appear before verse 20—and several which appear later in the story—are in fact quotations from a much later Pali text called the *Cariyā-piṭaka* (*Cp.*). The *Cp.* is one of the very latest works to rank as canonical. It contains thirty-five utterly mediocre Pali poems, most of them quite short, which recount lives—one life to one poem—in which the Buddha-to-be attained each of the ten perfections. Ten of the poems are devoted to the first Perfection, that of Generosity; and this section includes the story of Vessantara in fifty-eight couplets, by far the longest poem in the book. It is clear that this brief and pedestrian account is based on the *Vessantara Jātaka* much as we have it now; for example, it begins with verses which are closely modelled on some of those in our prologue. The *Cp.* gives a sentimentalized and pietistic account of the story, with injections of the supernatural which are typical of our prose stratum. Thus, when Vessantara and his family are banished and set off on foot, the old verse (verse 227) merely records that to reach the Cetans' city they went 'a long way'; the *Cp.*, on the other hand, destroys the poignancy by explaining that out of pity for the children supernaturals shortened the road so that they covered the journey within one day; the redactor of our prose uses this verse and embroiders upon it. Quotations from the *Cp.* are almost all introduced by the words, 'So it is said', and also obtrude because in that work the Buddha identifies himself so closely with Vessantara that, as the narrator, he uses the first person. Rather than dilate on the many differences in tone and content between the old verse stratum and the prose stratum, which includes the verses quoted from the *Cp.*, we have indicated by the layout of our translation what is prose and what is verse, and marked the eighteen borrowed verses[1] with a *Cp.* in square brackets; thus the interested reader can compare the two strata for himself.

In his edition of the Pali text, Fausböll makes a typographical differentiation not only between prose and verse, but also within the prose. A part of the prose, which he prints in smaller type, is a commentary in the strict sense on the verse, explaining its meaning by citing and explicating particular words. It is generally assumed that this word-commentary represents a more modern stratum than the prose narrative, though both are technically known in Pali as the *Jātaka commentary* (*aṭṭhakathā, aṭṭhavaṇṇanā*). Fausböll arranges his text on this assumption, while apologizing (in his *Preliminary Remarks* to volume vi), 'It is sometimes not easy to see, what belongs to the Commentary and what to the Text.' Indeed, in our text he seems to us at several places (pointed out in Appendix II) to print in the smaller type what belongs in the larger. But maybe this piece of stratification is entirely unjustified: we note that the verses from the *Cp.* receive no word-commentary. We consider unproven the assumption that the prose narrative and the word-commentary are of different authorship. Nevertheless, the word-commentary can hold no interest for the

[1] They are listed and discussed by Alsdorf, pp. 3–9. Our total of 18 includes p. 504 lines 11–12 = *Cp.* 25, which we include in our text, although Fausböll prints it as commentary.

general reader, so we have determined—perhaps arbitrarily—on a boundary between it and the prose narrative, and translated only the latter.

Whatever may be the correct stratification, we would remind the reader that like all *jātaka*s, even if to a lesser extent than most, the *Vessantara Jātaka* is not and never was complete in its verses; these must always have been supplemented by a prose narrative. For example, Vessantara's arrival at his mountain retreat is not mentioned in the verse, nor is Jūjaka's return to Jetuttara; to make the story intelligible some such narrations as those on pp. 519–21 and pp. 573–4 of Fausböll's text are indispensable. What is under discussion is the stratification and chronology of the text as we now have it.

As for an absolute date for this text, the best we can do is to say that the prose narrative cannot postdate the fifth century A.D., when the writing of the Pali commentaries is supposed to have been completed; it is probably rather earlier than that, because a doctrinal treatise, the *Milinda-pañho*, knows of the seven earthquakes, which are in the prose but apparently not in the verse, and because a Sanskrit version of the story, that in the *Jātaka-mālā* of Āryaśūra, probably dating from the third or the fourth century A.D., contains an incident in our prose which apparently arises from a misunderstanding of the old verse.

It is interesting to examine examples of such misunderstandings. First, the one taken over by Āryaśūra. When Vessantara sets out with his family from Jetuttara, he goes in a carriage drawn by four horses; but very soon four brahmins hurry up and beg the horses from him. At this point, says the prose, the yoke stayed in mid air, and four gods disguised as red deer came and yoked themselves to it. Vessantara draws attention to them, in a verse, and then immediately a fifth brahmin comes and begs the carriage off him. Then, the prose says, the gods disappeared—having, we may think, performed a footling miracle of singularly short-lived effect. Alsdorf has ingeniously explained it. Just before the first four brahmins arrive, Vessantara speaks a verse (213, our p. 32) pointing out to Maddī the beauty of the city they are leaving; then, after one verse (214) describing his gift of the horses, Vessantara says a couplet (215) of which the first line is almost identical with the first line of 213; the second line reads, 'Clever horses, the colour of red deer, carry me on.' But the word for 'colour' can also mean 'appearance'. Alsdorf suggests that verses 214 and 215 were transposed; the author of our prose version was puzzled that horses should be drawing Vessantara's carriage when he had just given them away, and misinterpreted or reinterpreted the words so as to make them refer to phantom steeds, or rather phantom deer.

This explanation appears to us convincing. The supernatural incident generated by a chance misunderstanding appealed to contemporary sentiment, and became embedded in the tradition. We add this rider, because we are somewhat worried by the free use that Alsdorf makes of the hypothesis of transposition. In several places he posits transpositions far more complicated than the above, in one case (text pp. 490–1) reshuffling four chunks of verse. All his rearrangements make the sequence of verses more logical, but we are not convinced that literature of this type is invariably logical. Moreover, it is unclear how such transpositions could have arisen. In no case does any manuscript support Alsdorf's rearrangement, so the transpositions must be ancient. Did they occur during oral or written transmission? Neither is easy to envisage. So popular a story could hardly have depended on a single line of tradition. Had a chance transposition due to a lapse in a reciter's memory or (most improbably) to a jumbling of manuscript leaves produced a garbled version of a well-known episode, and brought no benefits like the interesting red deer in compensation, we find it hard to believe that it alone would have survived. For this reason, despite their ingenuity, we have been chary of accepting Professor Alsdorf's conjectures of transposition.

Another misunderstanding of the verse by the author of the prose is not dependent on a hypothesis of textual corruption. When Vessantara gives away his children, he tells them in a prose passage (text pp. 546–7)—there is no verse on the subject—that if they wish to redeem their freedom Jāli must pay a thousand gold coins, while Kaṇhājinā's price is a hundred slaves, a hundred horses, a hundred elephants, etc. It seems odd to price the girl so much higher than the boy, and the author offers the transparently factitious explanation that Vessantara wishes to avoid an inter-caste marriage, and so sets a price which only a king could afford. Alsdorf has shown how the oddity arose. When the children, led by Jūjaka, come to Sañjaya's court, and he wishes to redeem them, he asks them (text p. 577) at what price their father valued them. Jāli replies (verse 671) that he was valued at a thousand, Kaṇhājinā at 'an elephant and a hundred'. The king is carried away by the emotion of the moment, and in the next verse (672) tells his steward to give Jūjaka 'a hundred female and a hundred male slaves, a hundred cows, elephants and bulls, and a thousand in gold'. A literal-minded redactor has tried to make the two verses harmonize by interpreting 671 as a brachylogy.

Finally, let us point out misunderstandings concerning proper names. The name of Vessantara is given a most palpable false etymology (text p. 485) as *vessa-antara*, 'among the *vessas*', i.e. [born] among the merchant class. The silly episode invented to justify this etymology is found also in the *Cariyā-piṭaka*. The etymology requires Pali, for the Sanskrit form of the name, Viśvantara, cannot be so punned upon. Alsdorf, following Jacobi, etymologizes Viśvantara to mean 'giving everything'—an ideal meaning and so an attractive theory, but unfortunately most improbable. In fact the name Viśvantara occurs already in a Vedic text, the *Aitareya Brāhmaṇa*, which probably dates from the eighth or ninth century B.C.; there it has nothing at all to do with our hero, but is the name of an otherwise unknown king called Viśvantara Sauṣadmana.[1] If Viśvantara meant anything to the originators of the story, the likeliest etymology is 'all-saving', for this meaning of *-tara* is attested in the *Mahābhārata*. But we rather think that the name had no significance. The name Mādrī occurs in the *Mahābhārata*, where it designates the mother of the twins Nakula and Sahadeva; it means 'daughter of the Madra king', the Madras being a north Indian people. That meaning has no relevance to our story; the name is just that of an epic character; and Viśvantara no doubt is similar.

Another misunderstanding seems to have given rise to the name

[1] *Ai. Br.* 7. 27. In his commentary Sāyaṇa etymologizes Sauṣadmana but not Viśvantara.

of Vessantara's magic elephant, Paccaya. Paccaya is a peculiar name for an elephant, because it is a common Pali word of which the commonest meaning is 'cause'. It also means 'a requisite', that is, property indispensably associated with a certain social status, such as a monk's begging bowl. When at the end of the story his father visits Vessantara in the mountains to recall him, he anoints him king and then they prepare the triumphal procession homeward. Verse 751 reads: 'When he was washed from head to foot and was wearing clean clothes and all kinds of jewellery, he mounted the proper elephant and bound on his sword, the scourge of his enemies.' 'Proper' here translates Pali *paccaya.* The word is a trifle unusual in this context, and has been misconstrued as a proper name.[1] As if this was not enough, the prose author has second thoughts, and when he first introduces the elephant (text p. 485) he gives yet another etymology of its name, having recourse to an idiom in which *paccaya* has its commoner meaning of 'cause'. Our interpretation is corroborated by the mysterious sixty thousand warriors, who are mentioned along with Paccaya as having been born on the same day as Vessantara, but play no part in the story. In the very next verse after Vessantara has mounted his proper elephant to return home, we are told that sixty thousand warriors of equal birth formed his retinue. The word *sahajātā*, 'of equal birth', literally means 'with-born', and has been misinterpreted to mean 'born at the same time [as Vessantara]'. The birth of Paccaya too on the same day has occurred by osmosis.

But the consequences of this misunderstanding go still further. In some later versions the magic rain-producing elephant returns at the end of the story. We submit that this did not happen merely through a desire for the happiest ending possible. The story-tellers found Paccaya back again at the finale, both in verse 751 (just cited) and in verses 754–6, each of which begin, 'For that reason . . .'; there the word *paccaya* is again used in the sense of 'cause', and with a little grammatical obtuseness the phrase can be misunderstood to mean, 'Having obtained Paccaya . . .' That

[1] Verse 751c, *paccayaṃ nāgam āruyha,* has been copied by *Cp.* 15c, where it applies to the elephant Vessantara is about to give away. One cannot tell how the author of *Cp.* understood the phrase. His commentator takes *paccaya* as the elephant's name, but then he bases himself on our *VJ* text.

the elephant's name is Paccaya only in Pali versions does not seem a grave objection to this theory, as the episode would be more likely to survive among speakers of other languages than a name which to them was meaningless; moreover, the earliest surviving version to report the return of the elephant, the Chinese, does seem ultimately to be based on our Pali text (see below).

From the internal development of the text, we turn to consider the story's diffusion.

There is hardly a major Buddhist site in India which has no representation of Vessantara. Vessantara's gifts of the elephant, his chariot, and his children were carved at Bharhūt (second century B.C.?), and the full depiction of the story on the north gate at Sānchī (first century B.C.) is famous. Among the carvings found at Amarāvatī (first to third centuries A.D.?), scenes from the story are shown in six places; and at Goli (third century A.D.?) a stone frieze measuring 7 ft. 6 in. × 11½ in. showed the story in eight scenes. The subject occurs several times in Gandhāran art. The wall of cave XVII at Ajaṇṭā (fifth century A.D.?) probably does not bear the oldest surviving paintings of the story, for Sir Aurel Stein discovered at Mirān in Chinese Turkestan a frieze of the *VJ*, originally 18 ft. long but partly destroyed, painted in Graeco-Buddhist style on a field of Pompeian red, and Professor A. D. H. Bivar dates it to the second century.[1] Nor should we neglect to mention the claim of the Ceylon chronicle, the *Mahāvaṃsa* (fifth century A.D.), that King Duṭṭhagāmaṇī *c.* 80 B.C. had the relic chamber inside the Great Stupa painted with scenes including the *VJ*;[2] but this painting, if it survives, is immured within the stupa.

Ancient literary evidence for the *VJ* is mostly even more difficult to date than that of the visual arts. The principal literary language of ancient India was Sanskrit (i.e. Old Indo-Aryan). Buddhism does not seem to have used Sanskrit, the classical language of Hinduism, for literary composition before the Christian era; and early Buddhist Sanskrit works tend to be written in a Sanskrit which reads like a translation from one of the Prakrits (i.e. Middle Indo-Aryan languages, such as Pali), which Buddhism

[1] Personal communication from Professor Bivar. [2] *Mhv.* XXX, 88.

more traditionally used. Aśvaghoṣa, the first known Buddhist author to use really 'correct' classical Sanskrit, probably dates from the second century A.D. The *Jātaka-mālā* of Āryaśūra probably shows his literary influence. Another work by Āryaśūra was translated into Chinese in 434; so the *Jātaka-mālā* probably dates from the third or fourth century A.D. In it Āryaśūra tells a number of *jātaka* stories in a mixture of prose and verse, recalling their original form; but here the whole is a unitary composition, fluent and polished. The story of Vessantara is included, with exactly a hundred verses. This version presupposes the *VJ* verses and much of the material in the Pali prose. King Sañjaya has a steward, called a *kṣattr* (= Pali *khattar*); Lüders pointed out, when writing of the Pali *Jātaka* verses, that this is an archaic term, dating from late Vedic–early epic times. This is but one of the verbal correspondences which show that Āryaśūra has borrowed directly from the Pali, or something extremely close to it; another example is the children's lament, which Keith in his standard *History of Sanskrit Literature* singles out for praise as if it were original, but which corresponds almost *verbatim* to our text. When Vessantara (to whom Āryaśūra generally refers as 'the Bodhisattva'—'the Buddha-to-be') has given away his horses, he prepares to yoke himself to the carriage, but the four spirits turn up in the guise of red deer.

In the early centuries A.D. Mahāyāna Buddhism arose, and became more popular in India, in central Asia, and the Far East than the older schools of Buddhism (which were collectively dubbed Hīnayāna), though its victory was only gradual, and in India never complete. As time went on, Buddhist literature attributed to the Buddha in his former lives ever more extravagant acts of self-sacrifice; by the standards of Mahāyānist hagiography Vessantara's gift of other people, a mere 'external gift', was by no means extreme. Indeed, Alsdorf suggests that the introduction of verses from the *Cariyā-piṭaka*, in which Vessantara in boyhood regrets the lack of opportunity to give away his own flesh, reflects an uneasy realization by latter-day Theravādins of these inflated standards. But the story of Vessantara suffered no decline in popularity.

Of this its literary diffusion is one indication; but there is also other evidence. The Chinese Buddhist Song Yun went on a pilgrimage from A.D. 518 to 522, in the course of which he visited a mountain in Gandhāra (an area now bisected by the border between Afghanistan and Pakistan). On this mountain he saw Vessantara's cave, with one entrance but two cells. Ten paces in front of the cave was a big square rock on which the prince had liked to sit; Asoka (he says) had built a stupa there. One *li* (very roughly a third of a mile) south of the stupa was the site of Vessantara's leaf hut; one *li* north-east of the stupa he saw the actual tree to which the children had clung, and a fountain which sprang from the spot on which their blood had fallen when they were beaten. Three *li* west of the dwelling Sakka took the form of a lion and barred Maddī's way; traces of his hair, tail, and claws were still visible on the rock. Stupas also commemorated the sites of Accuta's cave and the place where his disciples gave food to Vessantara and his family.

Song Yun also visited a town which Foucher identifies with modern Shāhbāzgaṛhī (in Pakistan). One *li* north of the town was a Buddhist temple commemorating the white elephant which Vessantara gave away. It was full of beautiful stone Buddha images covered with gold leaf. Before the temple he saw the tree to which the white elephant was tethered. According to a local tradition, when this tree died, the Buddhist religion too would die. Inside the temple was a painting of Vessantara and Maddī and the brahmin asking for their children, which none of the barbarians could look at without shedding tears.

In the next century the most famous of all the Chinese pilgrims, Hiuen Tsiang, visited Gandhāra on his way to India. He evidently saw the same sites as Song Yun, though his account differs in detail: for him the temple commemorated not the giving of the elephant but the spot where Vessantara bade his friends farewell as he departed for exile; and the stupa allegedly built by Asoka was no longer there, though its foundations were visible. The hill, Hiuen Tsiang records, was twenty *li* north-east of the town—not, we may think, a great distance for a journey into exile.

The remaining literary evidence must be treated more summarily. Perhaps the most interesting question concerns the relationship between the different versions; this is very hard to determine, because few Sanskrit versions have been published, and the non-Indian versions may have been translated from Sanskrit (or from a Prakrit) at one or more removes. For brevity we shall concentrate on names rather than the more colourful material of variations in the plot.

Two of our exhibits are only fragmentary: that in Tocharian, the most easterly Indo-European language, is confined to two fragments; that in late Khotanese (an Iranian language) consists of six strophes within a longer work, the *Jātaka-stava* ('Praise of the Buddha's former lives'), which was translated from a lost Sanskrit original in the late tenth century. The elephant here is called Rrājevarrdaṃ, which recalls *rājyavardhana*, 'bringer of increase to the kingdom', which is the Sanskrit equivalent of *raṭṭhavaddhana*, a stock epithet in our Pali version but not used by Āryaśūra; and no detail mentioned is incompatible with the Pali version. These two versions were found by archaeological expeditions in Chinese Turkestan, the latter, along with the Sogdian versian (see below), by Sir Aurel Stein at Tun-huang in a chamber closed since the early eleventh century.

Two distinct versions, both quite lengthy, survive in Tibet. One of them is in the *Kanjur*, the Tibetan version of the Buddhist canon, which was translated into Tibetan between the eleventh and thirteenth centuries.[1] It is still comparatively close to the Pali, though further away than Āryaśūra. The elephant's name is based on *rājyavardhana*, the king is called Viśvāmitra, and his son is called Viśvantara after him. A distinctive feature is the happy ending for Jūjaka, who receives his price for the children and gets off scot-free. When his friends and relatives say that he owes his good fortune to Vessantara, he replies, 'What have I to do with Prince Viśvantara? As I was born in the first caste, I have

[1] What seems to be the Sanskrit original of this Tibetan version was found at Gilgit and is being edited in Berlin. Two manuscripts of a Sanskrit version, apparently entitled *Viśvantara Avadāna*, which may or may not be the same text as the Gilgit one, are in the library of Tokyo University.

obtained the recompense of the world, and therefore have I become so wealthy.'

The Kashmiri scholar Kṣemendra included the Vessantara story in his 'Wishing Creeper of the Buddha's Heroic Deeds' in the early twelfth century. His brief account differs considerably from the other extant Indian versions, but all his idiosyncrasies, with trivial and uninteresting exceptions, are in the *Kanjur*. For example, both have Vessantara give away a fine carriage in a separate incident before he gives away the elephant, and both end with a prosperous and unrepentant Jūjaka (whom at this point Kṣemendra calls Jambuka, 'jackal'). This version thus reads like an extremely condensed and deplorably desiccated retelling of the *Kanjur* version—not presumably of the Tibetan itself, which is probably later, but of the Sanskrit text of which the Tibetan is a translation. The one complication is that while towards the end Kṣemendra, like the *Kanjur*, calls Vessantara's father Viśvāmitra, he introduces him as Sañjaya; this unexplained inconsistency shows that he was at least familiar with two sources. Kṣemendra's work was in turn translated into Tibetan in 1272.

The difficulty of establishing historical links is vividly shown by our next item, the version in Somadeva's 'Ocean of the Rivers of Story'. Somadeva, a Hindu (this is the only version known to us which is not by a Buddhist), wrote in Kashmir only one generation after Kṣemendra, and it is almost inconceivable that he did not know his work; yet his version is quite different. Here Vessantara is called Tārāvaloka, Starlight, and his father Moonlight; his children are made male twins, Rāma and Lakṣmaṇa. Despite these discrepancies, Maddī remains Mādrī, and the main episodes of the story are all in place, much as in the *Jātaka-mālā*. The major difference is that Somadeva, as a Hindu, omits all reference to Buddhism, and makes Starlight's motivation an overwhelming desire to present gifts to brahmins!

Although we now move back several centuries, our three remaining versions drift ever further from the original story. For his journey to China Vessantara changed his name to Sudāna, 'he of good gifts', which appears in Chinese as Siu-ta-na. The story of Sudāna was translated into Chinese between A.D. 388 and 407.

This version is immensely amplified and exaggerated; even episodes from the early life of the Buddha himself (Siddhārtha) have been conflated. Not that this is strange: the Sinhalese paintings model Vessantara's wedding on Siddhārtha's and in at least one cycle the analogy is extended so that during boyhood Vessantara levitates, as did Siddhārtha (see Plate 4 (*a*)). Sañjaya's Chinese name derives from Śibi; the elephant is called Siu-t'an-yan, perhaps from Sudāna-yāna, which in Sanskrit would mean 'Sudāna's vehicle'. At the end the rival king who asked for the rain-making elephant sends it back to Vessantara with rich presents and a message of regret, but Vessantara declines it: if one has fed someone a good meal one does not want him to vomit it back. The rival king is edified and reformed. Despite the additions, many passages in this Chinese version closely resemble the Pali verse stratum; as Alsdorf says, its Sanskrit original must have been close to the Pali.

The version in Sogdian, another Iranian language, which was found in Tun-huang, is also fairly long, though the text is not quite complete. This version is as extravagant as the Chinese, to which it bears some relation: the hero's name is now Sudāšan, his father's Šivi. The elephant, on the other hand, is now called Rājvart, which takes us back to the Sanskrit–Tibetan stream. The number of incidents of giving is further multiplied.

Most changed of all—though still unmistakably the same story—is the Tibetan play *Drimedkundan*, 'Endowed with all the purities'. According to Bacot, this play used to be acted in Tibetan monasteries, and had many variant versions; it was traditionally ascribed, though without foundation, to the sixth Dalai Lama (*fl.* *c.* 1700). The dialogue, in verse, was chanted, while professional actors mimed and danced; the episodes were connected by short prose passages rapidly read or recited by a special actor. The male parts were read by monks, the female parts by professionals. This play was also read, and Bacot writes, 'It is told that some stout spirits claim to read it without weeping. Put to the test, they put a bold face on it till the fifth page, grimace towards the seventh, and burst into tears from the tenth.'

Of many changes, the greatest is that the gift for which the hero is exiled is no elephant but a wish-giving jewel. (Was this originally a metaphor applied to the elephant?) A good and a bad minister represent the forces of good and evil; due to the exertions of the good, the hero's punishment is twelve years in exile. He bids farewell to his mother (as in the Pali and the Chinese), and sets off with his wife and *three* children. On his way into exile he gives his three elephants loaded with provisions to three brahmins who beg him for alms. Next, five beggars get their horses and carriages—he and his wife have a carriage with two horses apiece. Then three beggars ask for and receive his children. Finally, two more get his wife, but they turn out to be Indra, and restore her to him. All these donations happen on the way into exile. On the way home after twelve years, the hero gives a blind beggar his eyes (recalling the original King Sivi). But all ends happily, and in the end the hero passes on the kingdom to *his* children, and retires with his wife and the good minister to Ceylon, where he ends his days. This reminds us of the Pali version, to which we must now return.

The Pali scriptures were preserved in Ceylon throughout the first millennium A.D., and from Ceylon they passed to the rest of South-East Asia. For all this area, then, the version presented in this book is the basic one; local versions are derived more or less directly from it, and do not innovate.

There is no need here to catalogue the many retellings of the story in Sinhalese. Important for us is the *Vesaturu-dā-sanne*, 'Paraphrase of the *Vessantara Jātaka*', which the modern editor, Hettiaratchi, dates to 'somewhere about the twelfth century A.D.' (p. 70). This is primarily a word-commentary on the Pali verses of our text (including the verses borrowed from the *Cariyā-piṭaka*); there are also a few explanations of prose passages. The explanations very closely follow those of the Pali word-commentary, and so offer virtually no independent help towards a better understanding of the Pali; but occasionally the author has superior readings. These are referred to in Appendix II with the abbreviation Vds.

Our story is a favourite subject of Sinhalese folk ballads. Apart from versions telling the full story, we have in our possession quite recently printed pamphlets with poems, doubtless older, devoted respectively to Vessantara's marriage, his giving of the children, Jāli's lament, and Maddī's lament; there are certainly others. The Sinhalese do not have an old theatrical tradition, but a type of folk-opera called *nāḍagama*, which owes something to Western influence, sprang up in the nineteenth century—and sure enough, there is a *Vessantara Nāḍagama* (Sarachchandra: 102). From the *nāḍagama* developed the beginnings of a modern Sinhalese theatre. John de Silva (1857–1938) was a prolific and influential author; his genre, the *nurtiya*, was more like a Western musical than a straight play, and borrowed heavily from Indian theatrical tradition. Loosely constructed, his *Vessantara Jātaka Nāṭyaya* (see Plate 40 (*a*)) has a prologue and six acts, which are divided into nineteen scenes, and even so it gets no further than the restoration of Maddī to Vessantara. A film of Vessantara, *Vesaturu Sirita*, was made by D. C. L. Amarasinghe in 1965.[1]

In the Low Country of Ceylon it is common to recite the *VJ* at wakes. When people die in Ceylon, their bodies are laid out in their own homes and lie there for a couple of days before the funeral. During this time the relatives keep open house, and several people are up all night. There are men and women who visit such houses and recite the *VJ* in Sinhalese verse for hours at a time until dawn. They sit by the corpse and recite in pairs in very loud voices, chewing ginger or something else to keep from getting hoarse. They are not professional reciters, not organized and not paid; but they and all other visitors are given refreshments, so that the number of nights of recitation is partly determined by the resources of the bereaved. Such recitations may also take place in the week following the funeral. We interviewed one young man who recited regularly; a Low Country man now living in Kandy, he is importing the custom to the Up Country. He claims to have just picked up the poetry at wakes he attended. He recites the version called *Vessantara Jātaka Kāvyaya*, a late medieval ballad of about 700 stanzas, but he did not seem to have a very precise idea of its contents.

[1] We are grateful to Mr. Sunanda De Mel for this information.

The purpose of the custom, he said, was to dispel the grief of the mourners.

The ritual importance of the *VJ* is even greater in continental South-East Asia than it is in Ceylon. In Thailand, Laos, and Cambodia the main Buddhist festival of the year centres on its recitation. Tambiah tells us that in Thailand the *VJ* is known as *Mahachad*, 'the great *Jātaka*', and that Bun Phra Wes (Phra Wes = Vessantara) is the major annual ceremony of merit-making. The strictly religious event, which is accompanied by a fair and other more secular festivities, is the recitation of the *VJ*, which is to be completed within a day. It starts early in the morning and ends at about 8 p.m. There is first a sermon on the battle with Māra (see above, p. xviii), and then the *VJ* is recited in a version of a thousand verses—presumably our Pali text, which is so known (see translation, p. 6). 'First a Pali verse is recited; then the audience throws puffed rice at the Buddha image; then the monks tell the story in Thai' (Tambiah, 81). Similar festivities are reported in Cambodia by Leclère and in Laos by Karpelès. According to these latter authors, the recitation takes place in a temporary structure which is hung with cloth paintings (about twenty, writes Leclère) of the main scenes of the story. The festival takes place during the dry season, approximately in March; in Vientiane, according to Karpelès, it may happen once a month (for how many months?) beginning in the third Laotian month (approximately February), monasteries organizing it in rotation.

The most intensely Buddhist country by any quantifiable criteria—number of monks and monasteries, expenditure on religion per head—is Burma. In the preface to his retelling of the story based on the Burmese translation (of the Pali), Goss writes (p. ii) that

> paintings of the leading incidents of the tale have been and still are largely made use of in the decoration of the pagodas, monasteries, and rest houses of the land. The drama is a favourite one and its performance always attracts a large audience ready to spend the entire night in hearing of the trials of the prince and the devotion of his wife and children. It is sometimes played by children who are said to render some of the scenes, if anything, with greater effect than adult actors would hope to attain.

Spiro includes the *VJ* in what he calls (p. 359) 'the core of the monastic curriculum'. Elsewhere he writes (p. 108; see also pp. 346–7):

> Taught to every schoolboy, alluded to frequently in conversation, recounted repeatedly in sermons, and—even more important—regularly enacted in dramatic form as part of the standard fare of the Burmese repertory troupes, the story of Prince Vessantara is probably the best known and most loved of all Buddhist stories. Its sacrificial idiom provides the charter for and reinforces the Burmese belief in the religious efficacy of giving.

III

In discussing the popularity of the *Vessantara Jātaka* in South-East Asia we have so far mentioned the visual arts only in passing; but one of our aims in this book is to give the reader a glimpse of how the average Buddhist visualizes the story. Jātaka illustrations proliferate in centres of Buddhist civilization, such as Borobodur in Java (ninth century), Pagan in Burma (thirteenth century), and Sukhodaya in Thailand (fourteenth century). In one sense, therefore, we face an *embarras de richesses*. In another sense, however, there is a paucity of material, for little of this art is available in photographs.

We have decided to present the picture of the *Vessantara Jātaka* drawn for itself by one society, the Sinhalese; and in so doing to document for the first time a large number of paintings which seem intrinsically worthy of rescue from oblivion. So far as we are aware, only one of the works here reproduced, the mural shown in the frontispiece and Plates 22 (*b*) and 33, have ever been published before, and then not in colour. We have taken nearly four hundred photographs of Sinhalese depictions of our story, and here aim to present a cross-section of them, rather than to concentrate exclusively on the best. All but the last three plates are from Buddhist shrines, or 'temples', as they are locally called, and all but a few are mural paintings.

We mentioned above that a king of Ceylon is supposed to have had the subject painted in a shrine in the first century B.C.; it has remained a favourite ever since. However, the Ceylonese climate is not kind to temples or their paintings. Moreover, there was comparatively little achieved in Buddhist art or architecture during the early Kandyan period, the sixteenth and seventeenth centuries, when organized Buddhism was in severe decline. The Buddhist revival can be dated from the reintroduction of the higher ordination from Siam in 1753; and though few of the older works shown in this book can be securely dated, none of them is likely to be much older than this. Artistic standards began to decline after the fall of the Kandyan kingdom in 1815; however, certain craft traditions were maintained much longer, and some of the most gifted pictures here shown date from the nineteenth century. A more decisive break came in the twentieth century, with the intrusion of Western influence.

The traditional arts and crafts of the Sinhalese, especially of the up-country (Kandyan) Sinhalese, who retained their political independence till 1815, are fully discussed in Coomaraswamy's monumental work, *Medieval Sinhalese Art*, to which the interested reader may turn. Coomaraswamy is especially informative on the social context of the arts, on technical data (e.g. the composition of pigments), and on written traditions which guided the executants. In other respects, however, his chapter on painting is comparatively meagre, and the history of Kandyan painting unfortunately remains an uncharted field. The materials for such a history have by now nearly all disappeared, while most of the surviving paintings are in poor condition. It is quite possible that by the end of this century no Kandyan murals will be preserved. So quickly can a cultural tradition be lost forever.

Kandyan painting operated within rigid conventions, and yet within those conventions displayed an astonishing variety of styles, so that not even the most superficial observer can conclude that 'when you've seen one, you've seen them all'. The style is strictly linear: all figures and objects are outlined against a red background, and the details are carefully drawn in. Rigid conventions govern the use of colour, and the depiction of trees, buildings, deities, and costumes; landscape features are conventional almost to the point of appearing in symbolic shorthand. Empty spaces in the red ground tend to be punctuated by floral decorations, and there is a general attempt to fill the picture space, though this becomes more marked in later work. There is no perspective or shading, and the general effect is thus two-dimensional. On the other hand, there is great variety in the human and animal figures which generally dominate the scene. The human figure tends to be slim, even elongated, and is often shown making some eloquent gesture. Stories are depicted by showing the scenes in uninterrupted sequence without formal division, the same figures constantly reappearing as one scene flows into the next; but the figures are dramatically grouped, so that the narrative is usually easy to follow. Sometimes the viewer is also given labels or captions, either in or below the picture, to guide him. There is no set convention about whether stories read from left to right or vice versa; frequently they zig-zag down—or even up—a wall; and occasionally the painter even uses the same plane for two sequences, figures going one way intermingling with figures going the other way in an earlier episode. In depicting long stories, such as ours, painters with a fair amount of space at their disposal exercise a surprising amount of individual initiative in their selection of scenes; when only a couple of scenes are shown the selection is naturally more stereotyped.

The relation of Kandyan art to schools outside Ceylon is still unexplored. There is a tradition that the caste of Sinhalese craftsmen came from South India in medieval times; and because it is so close one would in any case look first to South India for relationships. But so little medieval South Indian painting has been published that the search is as yet hardly feasible. Some Tamil paintings do share the red background, but other similarities are not yet conspicuous. Still less, however, does Kandyan painting seem to be related to that of the nearest Buddhist countries, Burma and Thailand.

The originality of some fine paintings in the Low Country (Plates 2, 6, 10 (*b*), etc.) suggest the intrusion of some non-traditional influence already in the early nineteenth century. But unambiguous western influence first made itself felt at about the turn of the century. Some of its first products are curious, but not devoid of charm. In this Edwardian period, if we judge correctly, probably the last great Kandyan painter was at work: D. S. Muhandirama stands out as an individual in a largely anonymous tradition because he supplied much of the material for Coomaraswamy's book (op. cit., p. 79). (In one place, Telaṁbugala, work by Muhandirama and his delightfully original contemporary, the naïve 'master' of Plate 12 (*b*), etc., is even to be found within the same building.) Western influence made its greatest impact through Sarlis (Plate 38 (*a*)), who mastered perspective and realistic figure drawing in the classical Western manner. Although much of his work may strike us as sentimental, the technical competence is impressive. Sarlis became famous not so much because he painted two large temples in Colombo (for once without Vessantara) as because he flooded the market with his cheap prints. Few Sinhalese Buddhist homes used to be without one (and they were also exported to South-East Asia); now, however, original Sarlis prints are yellow with age, and to some perhaps appear old-fashioned in style, so that they have been widely superseded by unsuccessful imitations, with harsher colours and cruder drawing (Plate 38 (*b*)). Much the same goes for the painting of temples; it is the 'Low-Country' (Westernized) style which is prestigious all over the island, and this term implies not merely attempts at perspective, landscape drawing, and other stylistic features, but the use of modern materials, poster- and enamel-paints in garish colours. A 'Low-Country' innovation is the creation of painted tableaux, sculpted scenes from the *jātaka* stories etc. with free-standing figures, often life-size and always brightly painted (Plate D (*b*)). Earlier, statues were used to represent only the Buddha and, very occasionally, his chief disciples; all other subjects were painted on the walls. A few monasteries also possess paintings done on cloth or on paper; episodes from three cloth paintings are reproduced here.

THE PERFECT GENEROSITY OF PRINCE VESSANTARA

THE TEACHER told this story on the occasion of a lotus-leaf shower while he was living in the Banyan Grove near Kapilavatthu. For when the Teacher had set in motion the Wheel of the Excellent Dhamma, he next went to Rājagaha, where he spent the winter. Then on his first journey he went to Kapilavatthu accompanied by twenty thousand in whom the defilements had been destroyed, with the Elder Udāyi showing the way. 479

At that time the Sākyan chiefs assembled, thinking to see the greatest of their family, and deliberated about the place where the Lord should stay. Observing that the park of Sakka of the Banyan Tree was lovely, they gave complete directions for its care. Then they went out to meet him, carrying perfumes and flowers and such things, sending out first the young boys and girls of the city, adorned with all kinds of ornaments, and then the children of the chiefs. Among these they themselves escorted the Lord to the Banyan Grove, paying worship to the Teacher with perfumes, flowers, powders, and so on. And there, surrounded by his retinue of the twenty thousand in whom the defilements had been destroyed, the Lord sat down on the excellent appointed Buddha-seat.

Now the Sākyans are proud by nature and stubborn in their pride, and they thought: 'This Prince Siddhattha is younger than we are; he is our younger brother; he is our nephew; our son; our grandson.' So they said to the chiefs' sons: 'You pay homage to him, and we shall sit down behind you.' When they sat down without paying homage to him, the Lord saw their thoughts, and decided that as his relatives were not paying homage to him, then he would make them pay homage. So he entered that state of trance which is a basis for magical power and, getting up, he rose into the air. Then, as though sprinkling the dust from his feet on their heads, he performed the Miracle of the Pairs as he did at the foot of the Knotted Mango Tree.

When the king saw this miracle he said: 'On the day you were born, sir, when you were brought to pay homage to Kāḷadevala, I saw your feet turned round and placed on the brahmin's head, and then I paid homage to you. That was my first homage to you. Again, on the day of the ploughing-festival when you sat on the royal couch in the shade of a rose-apple, I saw that the rose-apple's shadow did not move round, and then I paid homage at your feet. That was my second homage to you. And now, when I see such a miracle as I have never seen before, I pay homage at your feet, and this is my third homage to you.' When the king had paid homage, not a single Sākyan could remain without paying homage, and they all paid homage to him.

When he had thus made his relatives pay homage to him, the Lord came down from the air and sat on the appointed seat. When the Lord was seated, the assembly of his relatives had been taught a lesson, and all sat down and paid attention. Then a great cloud rose up, and rained a lotus-leaf shower, and copper-coloured water poured down with a loud noise, and those who
480 wished to be made wet were made wet, while not even a drop
fell on the body of anyone who did not wish to be made wet.

The hearts of all there, when they saw it, were filled with wonder and amazement, and they began to say to one another, 'O what a miracle! O what a wonder! O the great power of Buddhas, on whose assembled relatives such a lotus-leaf shower has rained!'

When he heard this the Teacher said, 'This is not the first time, monks, that a great cloud has rained a lotus-leaf shower on my assembled relatives.' At their request he told them of the past.

ONCE upon a time the Great King of the Sivis, who was ruling in the city of Jetuttara, in the kingdom of the Sivis, had a son named Sañjaya. When Sañjaya came of age the king sent for a princess called Phusatī, who was the daughter of the king of the Maddas, and handing over the kingdom to him, he made her chief queen.

Here is the account of her previous lives.

Ninety-one aeons ago a Teacher called Vipassin was born in the world. While he was living in the deer-park Khema near the city of Bandhumatī, a certain king sent to King Bandhuma a golden necklace worth a hundred thousand gold coins, together with fine sandalwood beyond price. The king had two daughters to whom he decided to give this present, but when he gave the fine sandal to the elder and the golden necklace to the younger, they thought, 'We will not wear these things on our own persons, but we will use them to pay honour to the Teacher.' The king gave his approval when they told him that they intended to pay honour to the Lord of Ten Powers with the fine sandalwood and the golden necklace; and so the elder had the sandal powdered and had a golden casket filled with it, while her younger sister had a breast-ornament made from the golden necklace and had it placed in a golden casket. These they had taken when they went to the holy dwelling in the deer-park. The elder honoured the golden-coloured body of the Lord of Ten Powers with the sandal-powder, and scattered what was left in the Perfumed Hut where he lived. Then she made an aspiration: 'O sir, may I in the future become the mother of a Buddha like you!' The younger sister adorned the golden-coloured body of the Tathāgata with the breast-ornament made from the golden necklace, and made her aspiration: 'O sir, may this ornament never disappear from my body until I become Enlightened!' The Teacher gave his blessing to their prayers.

Having lived out their natural lives they both came into being 481
in heaven. The elder sister transmigrated between heaven and the world of men until after ninety-one aeons she became Queen Māyā, the mother of the Buddha. The younger sister, transmigrating in the same way, was born as a daughter of King Kiki in the time of the Lord of Ten Powers called Kassapa. Because when she was born it looked as though a golden breast-ornament had been painted on her chest, the girl was called Uracchadā [Breast-ornament].

When she was sixteen, hearing the Teacher give thanks for food, she achieved the result of one who has entered the Stream. Later, on the day her father too by hearing thanks for food achieved the result of one who has entered the Stream, she attained

Enlightenment. She took up the wanderer's life and passed away completely at death.

King Kiki had seven other daughters. Their names were:

> Samaṇī, Samaṇā, Guttā, the nun Bhikkhudāsikā, Dhammā, Sudhammā, and the seventh was Saṃghadāsī.

In the life of this Buddha they were:

> Khemā, Uppalavaṇṇā, Paṭācārā, Gotamā, Dhammadinnā, Mahāmāyā, and Visākhā as the seventh.

Of these Phusatī [Sprinkling] was the one called Sudhammā, and she practised liberality and other good deeds. Transmigrating among gods and men in a body which looked as though it were sprinkled with red sandal-essence, the result of the worship she had paid to the Buddha Vipassin with the sandal-powder, in course of time she came into being as the chief queen of Sakka, the king of the gods. At the end of her lifespan there, the five portents appeared, and Sakka the king of the gods realized that her allotted time there had run out. He went with her in great pomp to the Nandana Grove, and there, sitting on the side of the ornamented couch on which she lay, he granted Phusatī ten wishes; and asking her to choose, he spoke the first verse of this great Vessantara Jātaka, which is adorned with one thousand verses:

> 'Most beautiful and splendid Phusatī, shapely in every limb, choose ten wishes for whatever is dear to you on earth.'

482 Thus this exposition of the Teaching in the great Vessantara Jātaka was established in heaven.

She did not realize that she had to die, and so she was distracted when she spoke the second verse:

> 'King of the gods, I pay you homage. What have I done wrong, that you make me fall from this lovely place, as the wind topples a tree?'

Aware then that she was distracted, Sakka spoke two verses to her:

> 'You have done nothing wrong, and you are no less dear to me, but your merit is used up: that is why I speak to you in this way.

'Your death is at hand, and we will be separated. So accept these ten wishes which I grant you.'

When she heard Sakka's words she knew for certain that she must die, and choosing her wishes she said:

'All hail to you, O Sakka, lord of all beings. If you have granted me a wish, then may I live in the home of the king of the Sivis.

'O Fort-destroyer, may my eyes be dark, my eyebrows black; may I be dark-eyed like a doe. May I have the name of Phusatī there also.

'May the king obtain a son who will be open-handed in granting requests, and without avarice; who will have fame and good repute, and be honoured by rival kings.

'When I am carrying him, may my waist not be swollen, and may my womb not be swollen, but like a smooth and even bow.

'May my breasts not hang slack, O Vāsava; may I not go grey. 483
May dust not stick to my body. May I have the condemned set free.

'May I be chief queen there in the home of the king of the Sivis, which echoes to the cries of peacocks and herons, which is thronged with groups of lovely women, crowded with men-servants and maidservants, extolled by bards and panegyrists, and noisy with jewelled doorbolts and the summons to meat and wine.'

Sakka replied:

'O lady on whose every limb sits beauty, through my gift you will obtain all the ten things you have wished for, in the land of the king of the Sivis.'

With these words the king of the gods, Vāsava Sujampati the 484
Bountiful One, gave his blessing to the wish of Phusatī.

End of the verses about the Ten Wishes.

WHEN she had been promised these wishes, she fell from that state, and was conceived in the womb of the king of the Maddas' chief queen. Since at the time of her birth her body looked as though it were sprinkled with sandal-powder, on the day she was given a name they called her Phusatī. She grew up with a great suite of attendants, and by the time she was sixteen years old was of most exquisite beauty. Then the great king of the Sivis brought her for his son, the young prince Sañjaya, over whom he raised the umbrella of kingship, and making her highest in rank of sixteen thousand women, he set her in the place of chief queen.

So it is said:

[*Cp.*] Phusatī fell from that state and was reborn in a royal family; and in the city of Jetuttara she was joined in marriage with Sañjaya.

She was dear to Sañjaya and pleased him.

Sakka took note, and saw that nine of the wishes he had granted to Phusatī had taken effect. 'But', he thought, 'one, the promise of a son, is not yet fulfilled. I shall fulfil that wish for her also.'

At that time the Great Being was living in the heaven of the thirty-three gods, and his allotted time there had run out. Knowing this, Sakka went to him and said: 'Lord, it is time for you to go to the world of men. It would be fitting for you to take your reincarnation in the womb of Phusatī, chief queen of the king of the Sivis.' When Sakka had received his consent and that of the other sixty thousand sons of the gods who were due to fall from that heaven, he returned to his own dwelling. The Great Being fell from that state, and was conceived in Phusatī's womb, and the other sons of the gods were conceived in the homes of sixty thousand ministers. When the Great Being had entered her womb, Phusatī felt a pregnancy craving to have six almshouses built: at the four gates of the city, in the middle of the city, and at the gate of her palace; she conceived a desire to give gifts, every day to give away six hundred thousand gold coins. When the king learnt of her craving, he consulted soothsayers, and when they said, 'Great King, the queen bears in her womb a being whose pleasure is in liberality, who will never be sated with giving,' in
485 his joy he established largess in the way described. And from the time of the Bodhisatta's conception there was no limit to the king's income, for through the influence of his merit kings

throughout the whole of India, the country of the rose-apples, sent him presents.

When the tenth lunar month of her pregnancy was completed, the queen with the child in her womb, accompanied by her great suite of attendants, wished to look at the city, and told the king. The king had the city adorned like a city of the gods; and placing the queen in the finest chariot sent her on a tour encircling the city, keeping its centre to her right. As she reached the middle of the street where the Vessas lived the pains of labour seized her. They told the king, and he had a lying-in chamber erected, right there in the street of the Vessas, and had her taken to it. And there she gave birth to a son.

So it is said:

[*Cp.*] For ten months she carried me, and while she toured the city, in the middle of the Vessas' street, Phusatī gave birth to me.

When the Great Being emerged from his mother's womb he was quite clean, and he emerged with his eyes open. Even as he was emerging he held out his hand to his mother and said: 'Mummy, I want to give a gift; have you anything?' 'My dear child, give just as you like,' said Phusatī, and placed a purse of one thousand gold coins in his outstretched hand. The Great Being spoke as soon as he was born on three occasions: in his Ummagga birth, in this birth, and in his final birth. On the day he was given a name they called him Vessantara, because he had been born in the Vessas' street.

So it is said:

[*Cp.*] My name is not my mother's, nor comes it from my father, but I was born in the Vessas' street, and so I became Vessantara.

On the very day he was born, a female flying elephant brought for him a completely white young elephant, which is considered very auspicious, and left after placing it in the state elephants' stable. Because the elephant was born by reason [paccaya] of the Great Being, they called it Paccaya.

The king appointed for the Great Being sixty-four nurses with sweet milk, avoiding those with defects such as exceptional height, and had nurses given to the sixty thousand boys born at the same time. The Great Being grew up with these sixty thousand boys, surrounded by a great suite of attendants.

Now for him the king had a princely ornament made, worth one hundred thousand gold coins, which he gave to him. The Great
486 Being, who was at that time about four or five years old, took it off and gave it to his nurses, and would not take it back when they tried to give it to him. They told the king what had happened, but he said, 'What is given by my son is given well. Let it be a holy gift,' and had another ornament made. While he was still a child the prince gave away those ornaments to his nurses nine times.

When he was eight years old, while sitting on his bed, he considered: 'I give only gifts that are external to me; but they do not satisfy me. I want to give something of my very self. If someone were to ask me for my heart, I would split open my breast, take out the heart and give it. If someone were to ask for my eyes, I would tear these eyes out by the roots and give them. If someone were to ask for the flesh of my body, I would cut off the flesh from my whole body and give it.' While he thus in rapturous thought pondered on his nature, this earth, four myriads and two hundred thousand leagues thick, shook, trumpeting like a mighty elephant mad with rut; Sineru, the king of mountains, bent down like a wet bamboo shoot, and bowed like a dancer towards the city of Jetuttara; the sky, echoing the thunder of the earth, rained down a sudden sharp shower; the lightning flashed forth; the ocean swelled; Sakka, the king of the gods, snapped his fingers in approval; Great Brahmā cried 'Bravo!'; and all was in tumult right up to the heaven of Brahmā.

This is said:

[*Cp.*] 'When I was yet a boy, eight years from my birth, sitting in my palace, I pondered giving gifts.

[*Cp.*] I would cut open my body, and give my heart, my eye, my flesh, my blood, if someone were to ask me.

[*Cp.*] While I pondered on my unquaking steadfast nature, at that time the earth, wreathed in the woods of Sineru, quaked.'

By the time he was sixteen the Bodhisatta had attained complete mastery of all skills and crafts. His father wished to hand over the kingship to him, and after discussion with his mother sent to the family of the King of the Maddas and had brought the daughter of the prince's maternal uncle. She was called Maddī. Making her highest in rank of sixteen thousand women, he set her in the place of chief queen. Then he anointed the Great Being [as his viceroy] in the kingship. From the time when he was established in the kingship, the Great Being instituted a great donation by distributing six hundred thousand gold coins each day.

In course of time Maddī gave birth to a son, whom they called 487
Jāli, since he was received at birth on a golden net [jāla]. When he was starting to walk, Maddī gave birth to a daughter, who was received on a black hide [kaṇhājina], and was therefore named Kaṇhājinā.

Six times each month, mounted on the back of his richly caparisoned elephant, the Great Being inspected the six almshouses.

Now at that time there was a drought in the kingdom of the Kaliṅgas. The crops did not ripen and there was great famine, so that men, unable otherwise to survive, were taking to stealing. Stricken by the famine the people gathered together in the royal courtyard and shouted their discontent. The king heard, and asked what was wrong. When they explained the trouble to him, he dismissed them, saying, 'Very well, my dear subjects, I shall make it rain.' So he undertook the moral vows, and fasted, but he could not make it rain. Then he called the citizens together, and told them that although he had undertaken the vows, and observed a fast for seven days, he had not been able to make it rain. 'So what are we to do?' he asked. They answered, 'Vessantara, son of King Sañjaya in the city of Jetuttara, who loves giving, has a completely white lucky elephant, and wherever it goes, there is rain. So if your Majesty cannot make it rain, then send brahmins to ask for the elephant and to bring it back.' The king agreed to do this, and calling together the brahmins, he chose eight of them, gave them expenses for their trip, and sent them to ask Vessantara for the elephant, and to bring it back.

Eventually the brahmins reached Jetuttara and ate in an almshouse. Their plan was to ask the king for the elephant on the full-moon day, and so they covered and splattered their bodies with dust and mud, and went to the east gate at the time when the king would visit the almshouse. The king meanwhile, intending to inspect the almshouse, bathed early in the morning with sixteen pitchers of fragrant water, breakfasted, adorned himself, and then, mounted on his richly caparisoned elephant, went to the east gate. The brahmins however could not get a place there, so they went and stood on a raised spot at the south gate, and watched the king giving alms at the east gate. When the king reached the south gate, they stretched out their hands and cried, 'Victory to the lord Vessantara!' Seeing the brahmins the Great Being directed his elephant to where they stood, and it was seated on its back that he spoke this first verse:

488 'Brahmins whose nails and hair are grown long, whose teeth are stained, whose bodies are grey with dust, stretch out their right hands. What do they ask of me?'

When they heard this, the brahmins said:

'O you who bring prosperity to the kingdom of the Sivis, we ask a precious thing: Give us the marvellous elephant, the colossal beast with tusks like poles.'

Hearing this the Great Being thought, 'I want to give something of my very self, to give something like my head. They ask only for what is external to me. I will fulfil their wish.' And still mounted on the elephant he promised:

'I do not hesitate; I give what the brahmins ask: the tusked riding-beast, best of elephants, trumpeter in rut.'

The king, bringer of prosperity to the kingdom of the Sivis, his heart set on liberality, got down from the elephant's back and gave that gift to the brahmins.

The ornaments on its feet were worth four hundred thousand; those on its flanks two hundred thousand; the cloth under its belly one hundred thousand; the three nets on its back, one of pearls, one of gold, one of gems, three hundred thousand; the bells on its ears two hundred thousand; the rug on its back one hundred thousand; the jewel on its frontal lobe one hundred thousand; its three head-ornaments three hundred thousand; the ornaments at the roots of its ears two hundred thousand; those on its tusks two hundred thousand; the lucky jewel on its trunk one hundred thousand, and the ornament on its tail one hundred thousand; so that, not counting the priceless objects, the trappings on its body were worth two million, two hundred thousand. Then the mounting ladder was worth one hundred thousand, its feeding vessel
another one hundred thousand, so that so far it was worth two 489
million, four hundred thousand. But more, there were six priceless objects: the gem on the top of the umbrella; the gem on the crown of its head; a gem in the string of pearls; the gem on its goad; the gem in the pearls on the covering of the elephant's throat; and the gem on its frontal globe. In addition, the elephant itself was priceless. So there were seven priceless things including the elephant, and all this he gave to the brahmins. As well as that, there were the elephant's attendants, five hundred families in all, together with mahouts and keepers. When the gift was made there were earth tremors and so on just in the way described already.

In explanation the Teacher said:

> Then there was a terrifying thing, then there was something to make your hair stand on end; when the great elephant was given away, the earth shook.
>
> Then there was a terrifying thing, then there was something to make your hair stand on end; when the great elephant was given away, then the city was rocked.
>
> Then the city was in confusion, and there was much noisy shouting, when the great elephant was given away, the bringer of prosperity to the kingdom of the Sivis.

The brahmins received the elephant at the south gate, and, mounted on its back, made their way through the middle of the city surrounded by a large crowd. When they saw them the people cried, 'Hey brahmins, that is our elephant you are mounted on! Where are you taking our elephant?' But the brahmins said, 'The great King Vessantara gave us the elephant. Who are you?' and mocking the crowd with insulting gestures, they carried on through the city and went out by the north gate. The citizens by a turn of fate were angry with the Bodhisatta; they gathered at the gate of the royal palace and shouted their discontent.

In explanation the Teacher said:

There arose such a terrible noise, such a great uproar; when the elephant was given away, the earth shook.

There arose such a terrible noise, such a great uproar; when the elephant was given away, then the city was rocked.

There arose such a terrible noise, such a great uproar; when the elephant, bringer of prosperity to the kingdom of the Sivis, was given away.

490 Incensed by his donations, those who lived in the city informed the king.

So it is said:

Lords and princes, tradesmen and brahmins, mahouts and guards, charioteers and foot-soldiers,

All the country people and the assembled Sivis, when they had seen the elephant led away, told the king:

'Your son Vessantara is ruining your kingdom, Your Majesty! How could he give away our elephant, our elephant so honoured in the kingdom?

'How could he give away the colossal trumpeter, with tusks like poles, experienced on all battlefields, the all-white best of elephants?

'The rutting crusher of our enemies, covered with its white blanket, tusked, white as Mount Kelāsa, with its chowrie,

'Its white umbrella, its cushion, its keeper, its attendants; that noble bearer, royal mount? He gave that treasure to some brahmins!'

With that said, they continued:

'Now if one gave food and drink, clothes or a place to live, that would be a suitable gift, and quite worthy of brahmins.

'But how, Sañjaya, bringer of prosperity to the kingdom of the Sivis, could your son Vessantara, the chief of your race, give away the elephant?

'If you do not do what the Sivis tell you, I expect the Sivis will use force against you as well as against your son.'

When he heard this the king thought, 'They want to kill Vessantara!' and he said: 491

'Let my country perish, let my kingdom be ruined, I will not, at the command of the Sivis, exile the prince, innocent as he is, from his own kingdom; for he is my son, dear to my heart.

'Let my country perish, let my kingdom be ruined, I will not, at the command of the Sivis, exile the prince, innocent as he is, from his own kingdom; for he is my son, my very own.

'I would not harm him, for he is full of noble goodness. It would be shameful for me, and would cause great sin. How could I slay him by the sword, Vessantara, my own son?'

The Sivis said:

'Do not slay him by the sword; he does not deserve imprisonment. Banish him from the kingdom; let him live on Crooked Mountain.'

The king said:

'If that is the Sivis' will, I shall not oppose their wish. But let him stay this one night, and enjoy all pleasures.

'Then, as night grows pale and sunrise approaches, let the Sivis assemble, and banish him from the kingdom.'

'All right,' they said to the king's request, 'let him stay one night only.' He dismissed them; and so that he might convey the command to his son, he summoned a steward and sent him to him. He went obediently to Vessantara's house, and told him what had happened.

492 In explanation, there are these verses:

'Off you go, steward, hurry to Vessantara and say, "Your Majesty, the Sivis and countryfolk have gathered together in their anger at you.

'"Lords and princes, tradesmen and brahmins, mahouts and guards, charioteers and foot-soldiers, all the country people and the Sivis have assembled,

'"And as night grows pale and sunrise approaches, the Sivis in a body will banish you from the kingdom." '

So commanded by the king of the Sivis, the steward hurried off, and adorned with bracelets, well-dressed, powdered with sandal,

His head bathed, his hair still wet, wearing jewelled earrings, he reached the lovely palace of Vessantara.

There he saw the prince at leisure in his palace, surrounded by his ministers, like Vāsava among the thirty-three gods.

The steward hastened to Vessantara and said to him, 'I bring bad news, but do not be angry with me, lord of charioteers.'

After this greeting, the steward, now in tears, said to the prince, 'O great king, who fully supply all our wishes, you are my supporter. I have bad news to tell. May His Majesty give me courage!

'Your Majesty, the Sivis and countryfolk have gathered together in their anger at you. Lords and princes, tradesmen and brahmins,

'Mahouts and guards, charioteers and foot-soldiers, all the country people and the Sivis have assembled,

'And as night grows pale and sunrise approaches, the Sivis in a body will banish you from the kingdom.'

The Great Being said:

'Why are the Sivis angry with me? I do not see what I have done wrong. Tell me, steward, what reason have they for banishing me?'

493 The steward replied:

'Lords and princes, tradesmen and brahmins, mahouts and

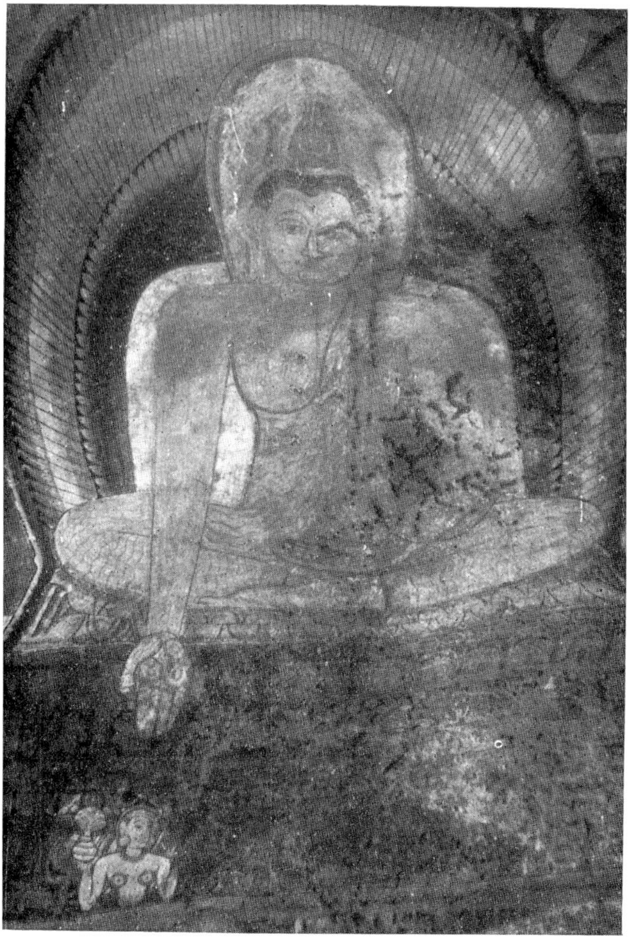
a

1. Painting on cave ceiling (plastered rock, uneven surface). Kabāllalena Raja Maha Vihāra, Vällāgala, Kurunegala District. Late eighteenth century?

(*a*) The Buddha calls the earth to witness his generosity.

(*b*) Māra is defeated and tumbles from his elephant. The *L.* side of this photograph overlaps with the bottom *R.* of (*a*).

b

2. The birth of Vessantara. Mural. Toṭagamuva Raja Maha Vihāra, Galle District. 1805.

3. Vessantara is installed as viceroy. Degaldoruva (see Pl. C (*a*)).

a

b

4. Mural. Dāḍigama Vihāra, Kegalle District. 1907.

(*a*) Vessantara levitates, worshipped by his parents (apocryphal episode).
(*b*) The marriage of Vessantara and Maddī. The two scenes are contiguous.

a

b

5. Hanguranketa—see C (*b*).

(*a*) Vessantara at home with his family.

(*b*) Vessantara gives away the elephant. The two scenes are contiguous.

a

b

6. (*a*) Vessantara gives away the elephant; on the *R.* is an almshouse. Mural. Käḷaṇiya Raja Maha Vihāra, Colombo District. 1888.

(*b*) Vessantara gives away the elephant. Toṭagamuva (see 2).

a

b

c

7. (*a*) Vessantara gives away the elephant. Mural on plastered rock. Dam̆bulla Raja Maha Vihāra, Matale District. Mid eighteenth century.

(*b*) The brahmins take the elephant off to Kalinga. Mural. Bam̆baragala Raja Maha Vihāra, Vaḍuvāva, Kurunegala District. Early twentieth century?

(*c*) The citizens complain to King Sañjaya. Same site as 7 (*b*).

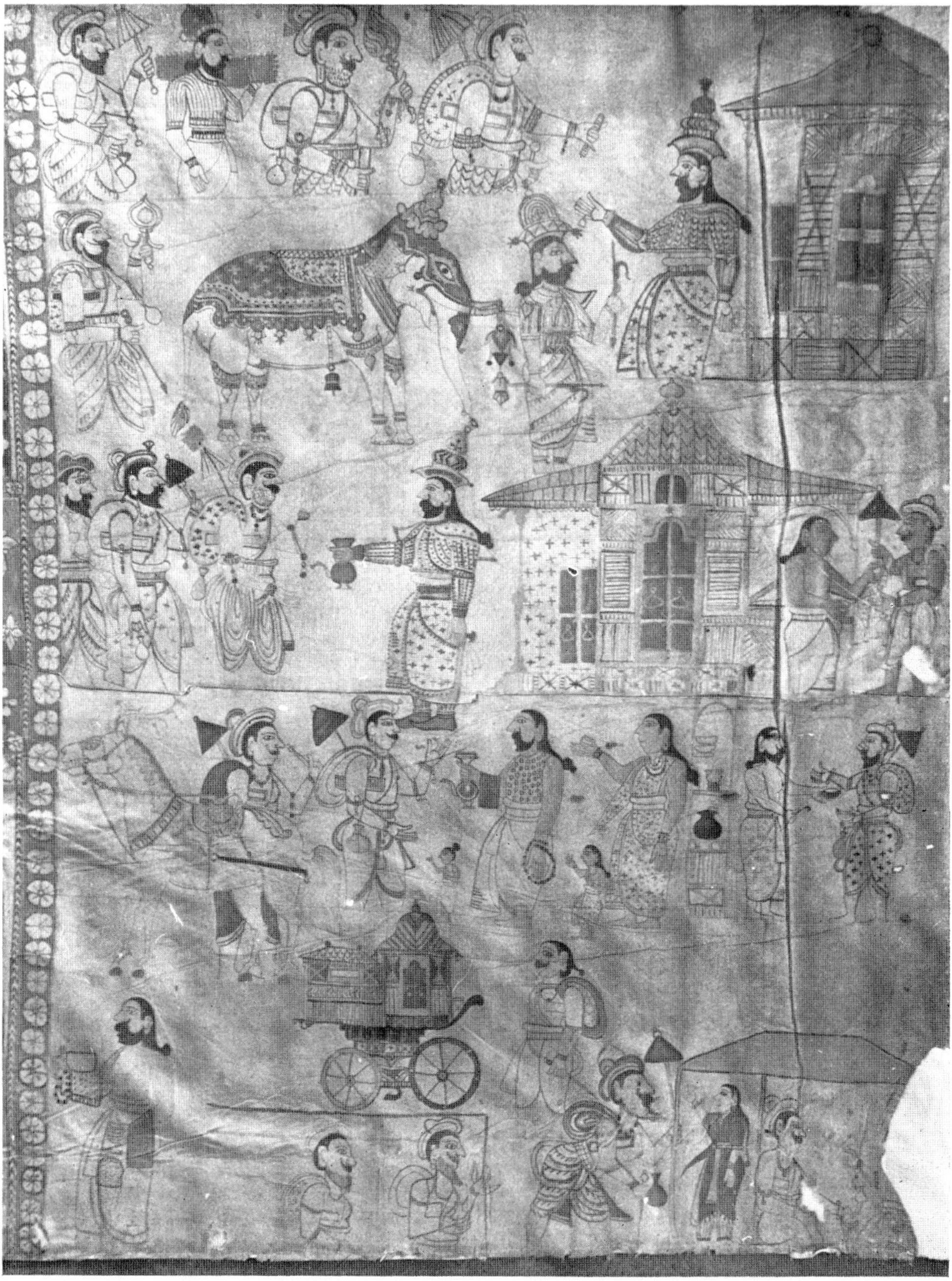

8. *Top half*: Vessantara gives away the elephant. *Bottom half*: he gives away horses and carriage and, on the right, food. *Bottom R. corner*: Jūjaka is sent on his way by his wife. Painting on cloth. Agrabodhi Vihāra, Dehipāgoḍa, Kandy District. Early twentieth century. Possibly by D. S. Muhandirama, who painted in the shrine at this temple.

guards, charioteers and foot-soldiers are angry because the elephant was given away, and that is why they are banishing you.'

When he heard this the Great Being was filled with joy and said:

'I would give my heart, or my eye! What is external wealth to me? What is gold or money or pearls or lapis lazuli gems?

'If I met anyone who asked for it, I would give my right arm and not hesitate. My mind delights in giving!

'Let the Sivis, all of them, banish me—or kill me! Let them cut me up into seven pieces, I will not stop giving!'

At this the steward spoke, not the message given him by the king, nor one given by the citizens, but different instructions from his own thoughts:

'The Sivis and the assembled country people say this to you: "Let the lord of good vows go where the exiled go, to Mount Ārañjara by the bank of the Kontimārā river." '

It seems he said this under the influence of a divine spirit. To his words the Bodhisatta replied, 'Very well. I shall go by the way taken by criminals, although the citizens banish me for no other crime than that I made a gift of the elephant. That being so, I shall make the great gift of the seven hundreds. If the citizens allow me to perform this gift for one day, after giving it tomorrow, I shall leave on the next day.

'I shall go where the malefactors go. Bear with me for 494
a night and a day, until I have given this gift.'

When the steward had said he would tell the citizens, he was dismissed and left. The Great Being then had the commander of the army summoned: 'Tomorrow I will give what is called the gift of the seven hundreds. Get ready seven hundred elephants, seven hundred horses, seven hundred chariots, seven hundred women, seven hundred cows, seven hundred female slaves, and seven hundred male slaves, and supply various kinds of food and drink, and even spirits—everything of a quality fit to be presented.' So having made arrangements for the great gift of the seven hundreds, he dismissed the ministers and went alone to Maddī's living-quarters, where he sat on the royal bed and began to talk to her.

In explanation the Teacher said:

The king told Maddī, on whose every limb sat beauty, 'Whatever I have given you, in money and grain,

'Gold or coins, pearls or lapis lazuli stones in plenty; store all of that, together with your own wealth which you have from your father.'

The Princess Maddī, on whose every limb sat beauty, asked him, 'Answer this question, Your Majesty: where should I store it?'

Vessantara said:

'You should give gifts to the virtuous, Maddī, as they deserve; for there is no surer foundation for living beings than making gifts.'

495 She acquiesced, saying, 'Very well,' and he instructed her further:

'Maddī, be kind to the children, and to your father- and mother-in-law. Wait respectfully on whoever puts himself forward as a husband for you.

'If no one comes forward, when I am far away, look for another husband, and do not waste away without me.'

Wondering why Vessantara spoke in such a way, Maddī asked, 'My lord, why do you speak so oddly?' The Great Being replied, 'The Sivis are angry because I gave away the elephant, and so they are banishing me from the kingdom. Tomorrow I shall give the great gift of the seven hundreds, and on the next day I shall leave the city.

'I go to the terrible forest, infested with fierce wild beasts. My life is at risk alone in the great forest.'

The princess Maddī, on whose every limb sat beauty, said to him, 'Why do you say this extraordinary thing? That is a wicked thing to say.

'It is not right, great king, for you to go alone. Where you go, sir, I go also. If the choice is death with you or life without you, such a death is better than living without you.

'It is better to die on a flaming fire, one blazing mass, than to live without you.

'Just as the cow-elephant follows her mate, the tusked 496
jungle-elephant, as he goes on his conquering way over mountains and difficult passes, the rough places and the smooth,

'So I shall follow behind you with our children. I will be no trouble to you; I will not be a burden.'

Then she described the Himālaya region as though she had already seen it:

'Seeing these children, sweetly chattering with their dear voices, sitting among the bushes of the forest, you will forget kingship.

'Seeing these children, sweetly chattering with their dear voices, playing among the bushes of the forest, you will forget kingship.

'Seeing these children, sweetly chattering with their dear voices in the lovely hermitage, you will forget kingship.

'Seeing these children, sweetly chattering with their dear voices, playing in the lovely hermitage, you will forget kingship.

'Seeing these children, adorned and hung with garlands in the lovely hermitage, you will forget kingship.

'Seeing these children, adorned and hung with garlands, playing in the lovely hermitage, you will forget kingship.

'When you see the children, hung with garlands, dancing in the lovely hermitage, you will forget kingship.

'When you see the children, hung with garlands, dancing and playing in the lovely hermitage, you will forget kingship.

'When you see an elephant, a trumpeter of sixty years, wandering alone in the jungle, you will forget kingship.

'When you see an elephant, a trumpeter of sixty years, wandering at evening and in the morning, you will forget kingship.

497 'When the elephant, the trumpeter of sixty years, trumpets out as he leads a herd of young elephants, when you hear his roaring, you will forget kingship.

'When you see the wild blossoms in the wood which is crowded with beasts of prey on every side, granter of desires, you will forget kingship.

'When you see the pañcamāli deer come at evening, and the fauns dancing, you will forget kingship.

'When you hear the murmur of the river as it flows, and the singing of the fauns, you will forget kingship.

'When you hear the cry of the owl as it flies hooting through the caverns of the mountain, you will forget kingship.

'When you hear in the forest the beasts of prey, the lion, the tiger, the rhinoceros, the buffalo, you will forget kingship.

'When you see the peacock with its tail-feathers dancing on the heights surrounded by the peahens, you will forget kingship.

'When you see the peacock with brilliantly coloured tail, born from an egg, dancing surrounded by the peahens, you will forget kingship.

'When you see the crested peacock with dark blue neck, dancing surrounded by the peahens, you will forget kingship.

'When you see the trees blossoming in the winter, spreading their fragrance, you will forget kingship.

'When you see the trees blossoming in the winter, the kuṭaja, and the flowering bimba tree, and the red lotuses, diffusing their fragrance, you will forget kingship.

'When in a winter month you see the earth green and covered with cochineal beetles, you will forget kingship.

'When you see the forest in bloom in a winter month, and the lotuses in bud, you will forget kingship.'

498 In just so many verses Maddī described the Himālayas, as clearly as if she lived there.

End of the Description of the Himālayas.

QUEEN PHUSATĪ, knowing the harsh command which had been given to her son, decided to go to him to find out what he intended to do. She went in a covered vehicle, and standing at the door of the royal room, she heard their conversation, and grieved deeply.

In explanation the Teacher said:

That famous king's daughter lamented piteously when she heard what her son and daughter-in-law said to one another.

'It would be best for me to take poison, or throw myself from a precipice, or strangle myself with a rope. Why do they banish my son Vessantara when he is guilty of no crime?

'Why should they banish my son Vessantara, who is so learned, so open-handed in granting requests, and without avarice; honoured by rival kings, renowned and famous? Why, when he is guilty of no crime?

'Why should they banish my son Vessantara, a man who supports his parents and pays due respect to the elders of the family, when he is guilty of no crime?

'Why should they banish my son Vessantara, who helps the king, the queen, his friends and relations, who helps the whole kingdom? Why, when he is guilty of no crime?'

So she mourned; and when she had spoken words of com- 499
fort to her son and daughter-in-law she went to the king and said:

'Like honey that has drained away, like mangoes fallen to the ground, so will your kingdom be, if they banish one who is guilty of no crime.

'Like a goose with crippled wings in a dried-up pond, you will be left alone, O king, deserted by your councillors.

'I say this to you, great king; let my meaning not escape you: Do not banish an innocent man at the bidding of the Sivis.'

To this the king answered:

'I act honourably according to my duty in chastising the emblem of the Sivis. I banish my own son, who is dearer to me than life itself.'

When she heard this, the queen wept and said:

'He who in earlier days was followed wherever he went by banners like blossoming kaṇikāras, today will go alone.

'He who in earlier days was followed wherever he went by banners like a forest of kaṇikāras, today will go alone.

'He who in earlier days was followed wherever he went by an array of troops like blossoming kaṇikāras, today will go alone.

'He who in earlier days was followed wherever he went by an array of troops like a forest of kaṇikāras, today will go alone.

500 'He who was followed as he went by the Gandhārans with their woollen robes, shining like the cochineal beetle, today will go alone.

'He used to travel on an elephant, in a palanquin, in a chariot: how will King Vessantara travel today on foot?

'How will one whose body is always anointed with sandal-paste, who is awoken with singing and dancing, wear the rough antelope skin of the ascetic? How will he carry the axe and pingo-load?

'Why do they not bring the saffron robes, or the antelope skins? Why do they not bind on the bark shirt as he enters the great jungle?

'How can they wear clothes made of bark, these people exiled by the king? How will Maddī wear a dress made of kusa grass?

'She is used to wearing fine cloth from Benares and linens from Kodumbara. How will Maddī manage when she has to wear clothes made of kusa grass?

'When she has travelled in litters, in a palanquin, in a chariot, how can that graceful girl make her way today on foot?

'That graceful girl, whose hands are tender, whose feet are always in comfort: how can that timid one go to the forest today?

'That graceful girl's feet are always in comfort, and the soles of her feet are so tender that even her golden slippers are oppressive to her as she walks: how can she make her way today on foot?

'She usually walks garlanded and attended by a thousand women: how can that graceful one make her way to the forest today all alone?

'She was immediately terrified, even inside her home, when she heard a jackal howl: how can that graceful one, timid as she is, go to the forest today?

'When she heard the shriek of the owl, that kinsman of Indra, in her terror at the noise she shook like the goddess of drink: how can that graceful one, timid as she is, go to the forest today?

'Like a bird whose chicks are killed, who sees the empty nest, so I shall waste away with the long sorrow, when I come to this empty home.

'Like a bird whose chicks are killed, who sees the empty 501
nest, I shall grow pale and thin, deprived of the sight of my precious children.

'Like a bird whose chicks are killed, who sees the empty nest, I shall run this way and that, deprived of the sight of my precious children.

'Like an osprey whose young are killed, who sees the empty nest, I shall waste away with the long sorrow, when I come to this empty home.

'Like an osprey whose young are killed, who sees the empty nest, I shall grow pale and thin, deprived of the sight of my precious children.

'Like an osprey whose young are killed, who sees the empty nest, I shall run this way and that, deprived of the sight of my precious children.

'So, like a ruddy goose in a dried-up pond, I shall waste away with the long sorrow, when I come to this empty home.

'So, like a ruddy goose in a dried-up pond, I shall grow pale and thin, deprived of the sight of my precious children.

'So, like a ruddy goose in a dried-up pond, I shall run this way and that, deprived of the sight of my precious children.

'If in spite of my bitter cries you banish the prince from the kingdom to the forest, when he is guilty of no crime, then I think I shall die!'

502 In explanation the Teacher said:

> When they heard her lament a noise rose up in the harem: the Sivi girls together stretched out their arms and cried aloud.
>
> Like sal trees uprooted and overthrown by the wind, wives and children lay prostrate in Vessantara's palace.
>
> Then, as night grew pale, towards sunrise, Vessantara the king began his gift-giving.
>
> 'Give clothes to those who want them, toddy to the drinkers! Give food to those in need of it. Give presents freely!
>
> 'Let no one cause difficulties to any beggars who have arrived here. Give them their fill of food and drink, so that they may go on their way properly honoured!'

504 So he gave the great gift of the seven hundreds: seven hundred elephants hung with gold, with golden standards, and covered with golden nets; seven hundred horses adorned likewise; seven hundred chariots spread with skins of lions and other beasts, brilliant with many kinds of gems, flying banners of gold; seven hundred women of the kṣatriya and other castes, wearing all kinds of adornments, and of supreme beauty; seven hundred well-trained and well-taught female slaves; seven hundred male slaves with the same qualities; seven hundred cows mated with the best bulls, each yielding a pailful of milk; and limitless food and drink.

As he gave the gift in this way, the inhabitants of the city of Jetuttara, from all four orders of society, cried, 'Lord Vessantara, those who live in the Sivi kingdom are banishing you because of your gifts, and yet you are giving away even more.' So it is said:

> [*Cp.*] Then there arose such a frightful noise, such a great uproar: 'It is because of your gifts that they are banishing you, but you have given yet more gifts!'

When they had had their gifts, the recipients thought, 'Now that King Vessantara has left us without support and gone into the jungle, to whom shall we go in the future?' And falling as though their feet had been cut off, they rolled to and fro, wailing very pitifully. And it was concerning this that the Teacher said:

So the beggars, tired and weary, gathered at the departure 502
of the great king, who brought prosperity to the kingdom of the Sivis.

'They have cut down a sturdy tree bearing all kinds of fruit, in banishing Vessantara from the kingdom, although he is guilty of no crime.

'They have cut down a strong tree, a fulfiller of every desire, in banishing Vessantara from the kingdom, although he is guilty of no crime.

'They have cut down a tree which brought the pleasures of all one's desires, in banishing Vessantara from the kingdom, although he is guilty of no crime.'

Old and young, and the middle-aged, stretched out their arms and cried aloud at the departure of the great king, who brought prosperity to the kingdom of the Sivis.

The overseers, the eunuchs, and the women of the king's harem stretched out their arms and cried aloud at the departure of the great king, who brought prosperity to the kingdom of the Sivis.

All the women who were there in that city cried aloud at the departure of the great king, who brought prosperity to the kingdom of the Sivis.

The brahmins, the wandering ascetics, and the other mendicants stretched out their arms and cried aloud: 'It is not right,

'The way Vessantara the king, making a sacrifice in his own city, is driven out of his own kingdom at the bidding of the Sivis!

'As he is driven out of his own kingdom, see, King Vessantara 503
gives away seven hundred elephants, the beast of independent will, wearing every sort of ornament, with golden harness and golden trappings, ridden by village headmen carrying pikes and goads.

'As he is driven out of his own kingdom, see, King Vessantara gives away seven hundred horses, swift steeds from the Sindh, thoroughbreds by birth, decked with every sort of ornament, ridden by village headmen carrying short-swords and bows.

'As he is driven out of his own kingdom, see, King Vessantara gives away seven hundred chariots, fully accoutred, with banners fluttering high, covered with leopard skins and tiger skins, bearing every sort of ornament, driven by village headmen in armour with bows in their hands.

'As he is driven out of his own kingdom, see, King Vessantara gives away seven hundred women with long lashes and charming smiles, graceful hips and slender waists, each standing in a chariot; who, arrayed in golden necklaces, embellished with gold, their dresses and trinkets the colour of gold, are completely adorned with gold.

'As he is driven out of his own kingdom, see, King Vessantara gives away seven hundred cows, each with a bronze milking-pail.

'As he is driven out of his own kingdom, see, King Vessantara gives away seven hundred female slaves and seven hundred male slaves.

'As he is driven out of his own kingdom, see, King Vessantara gives away elephants and horses and chariots and beautifully adorned women.'

Then there was a terrifying thing, then there was something to make your hair stand on end: when the great gift had been given, the earth shook.

Then there was a terrifying thing, then there was something to make your hair stand on end, when the king, his hands humbly folded, was driven out of his own kingdom.

505 Divine beings told kings throughout India, the country of the rose-apples, that Vessantara was giving a great gift of noble women and other things, and so, through this divine intervention, noblemen came by carriage and took away a noble woman or some other gift. People from all four orders of society went off with gifts from him, and at evening he was still giving.

When he had returned to his own home he thought, 'I shall take leave of my mother and father, and tomorrow I shall go away.'

So he went to his parents' home in a richly decked carriage and with him went Queen Maddī, who accompanied him so that she might get permission of her mother- and father-in-law to go. When the Great Being had greeted his father, he told him that he was going.

In explanation the Teacher said:

He said to King Sañjaya, best of the righteous, 'As you are banishing me, Your Majesty, I am going to Crooked Mountain.

'For all who have been, and all who shall be, go to the realm of Yama unsatisfied by material pleasures.

'I have troubled my own people, making a sacrifice in my own city, and so I am banished from my kingdom at the bidding of the Sivis.

'I shall endure this misfortune in the forest, the home of fierce wild beasts, the haunt of the rhinoceros and the leopard. I am doing good deeds; you sink in the mud.'

When he had spoken these four verses to his father, the Great Being went to his mother and asked her leave to go from home:

'Give me leave, dear mother, for I have decided to go from home. I have troubled my own people, making a sacrifice in my own city, and so I am banished from my kingdom at the bidding of the Sivis.

'I shall endure this misfortune in the forest, the home of 506
fierce wild beasts, the haunt of the rhinoceros and the leopard. I am doing good deeds; you sink in the mud.'

In answer Phusatī said:

'I give you leave, my son: prosper in your homeless life. But let the beautiful Maddī, whose hips are graceful and whose waist is slender, stay here with your children; for what will she do in the jungle?'

Vessantara said:

'I would not venture to take even a slave into the jungle against her will. If she wishes, let her follow me; if not, let her stay here.'

When he heard his son say this, the king began to plead with her. In explanation the Teacher said:

Then the great king began to plead with his daughter-in-law: 'Do not cover with muddy dirt and dust your body which is used to sandal-powder.

'You have worn Benares cloth: do not put on a dress of kusa grass. There is no joy in living in the jungle. O lady blessed with beauty, do not go!'

Then the princess Maddī, on whose every limb sat beauty, answered, 'I would not wish for any joy that was without my Vessantara.'

The great king, the bringer of prosperity to the kingdom of the Sivis, said to her, 'Come, Maddī, listen to what unbearable things there are in the forest:

'Many bugs and insects, mosquitoes and bees. They would hurt you, it would be very unpleasant for you.

507 'Take note of other tormentors which keep close to rivers: those snakes called goat-swallowers, which have no poison but are of great strength;

'They entwine in their coils any man or animal that may come near them, and so overpower them.

'And there are more: those black-furred animals which bring trouble, called bears. Once seen by them a man cannot escape even by climbing a tree.

'And there are buffaloes wandering there by the river Sotumbara, striking and clashing together their sharp-pointed horns.

'When you see the herds of wild cattle wandering in the forest, like a cow hankering after its calf, what will you do, Maddī?

'When you see the frightful monkeys gathered together in the tree-tops, as it will all be new to you, Maddī, you will be terrified.

'You are constantly terrified, even inside your own home, when you hear a jackal howl. What will you do, Maddī, when you get to Crooked Mountain?

'Even at midday when the birds are settled down together, the great jungle is full of noise. Why do you wish to go there?'

Then the princess Maddī, on whose every limb sat beauty, said to him, 'I will be able to bear all these terrors of the forest you describe. I shall go, O lord of charioteers.

'I will breast [the sea of] kāsa reeds, kusa and poṭakila grass, 508
usīra roots, munja and babbaja grass, and bulrushes. I will not be a burden for him to take along.

'A woman obtains a husband by many kinds of behaviour; by holding in her figure with corsets and stays of cow-bone,

'By tending the sacred fires, by sweeping out with water; for the life of a widow is a bitter fate in this world. I will go, O lord of charioteers.

'A man can take her by the hand and pull her around against her will, though he may be unworthy even to eat her leavings. The life of a widow is a bitter fate in this world. I will go, O lord of charioteers.

'He can pull her up by her hair, or drag her on the ground, and having caused her much grievous suffering, he does not remedy it. The life of a widow is a bitter fate in this world. I will go, O lord of charioteers.

'The white-skinned sons of a widow, arrogant in their good fortune, give her a pittance, and then pull her around against her will as crows mob an owl. The life of a widow is a bitter fate in this world. I will go, O lord of charioteers.

'Even if she lives with prosperous relations, rich in bronze, she does not escape abuse from her brothers and from the other women of the family. The life of a widow is a bitter fate in this world. I will go, O lord of charioteers.

'A river without water is bare; a kingdom without a king is defenceless; and bare and defenceless is a woman who is a widow, even if she has ten brothers. The life of a widow is a bitter fate in this world. I will go, O lord of charioteers.

'The banner marks the chariot; smoke is the sign of fire; the king symbolizes the kingdom; a husband gives meaning to a woman. The life of a widow is a bitter fate in this world. I will go, O lord of charioteers.

'That woman is honoured who shares the poverty of her

husband as well as his riches. The gods praise her, for what she does is hard.

'I will follow my husband always, wearing the yellow robes, for without Vessantara I would not want even the whole earth. The life of a widow is a bitter fate in this world. I will go, O lord of charioteers.

'Without Vessantara I would not want even the great wealth-bearing earth bounded by the ocean, full of all kinds of gems.

'What sort of heart have they got, those callous women who can wish for their own comfort while their husbands are suffering?

'I shall follow at his departure the great king, the bringer of prosperity to the kingdom of the Sivis, for he can satisfy all my wants.'

509 The great king said to Maddī, on whose every limb sat beauty, 'When you go, lady blessed with beauty, entrust these children, young Jāli and Kaṇhājinā, to us, and we will look after them.'

The princess Maddī, on whose every limb sat beauty, answered, 'My children Jāli and Kaṇhājinā are very precious to me, my lord; they will bring pleasure into our sorrowful life in the jungle.'

510 The great king, who brought prosperity to the kingdom of the Sivis, went on, 'The children are used to eating pure and excellent rice, with rich meat sauces: how will they manage when they have to eat berries?

'The children are used to eating from dishes of finest bronze, and from pure gold plate: how will they manage when they have to eat from leaf platters?

'The children are used to wearing fine cloth from Benares and linen from Kodumbara: how will they manage when they have to wear clothes woven from kusa fibres?

'The children are used to travelling about in litters, in a palanquin, or in a carriage: how will they manage when they have to run round on foot?

'The children are used to sleeping in a snug gabled house,

with door-wings securely bolted: how will they manage when they have to sleep at the foot of a tree?

'The children are used to sleeping on a couch, spread with woollen covers and brightly coloured cloths: how will they manage when they have to sleep with grass as their only bed and covering?

'The children are used to fragrant aloe and sandal rubbed on their bodies: how will they manage when they are covered with dust and muddy dirt?

'They lived in comfort, fanned by chowries and peacocks' tails: how will the children manage when they are bitten by flies and mosquitoes?'

As they talked the night grew pale; when the night sky was light, the sun rose. The Great Being's ornamented carriage, yoked with four Sindh horses, was brought and set at the entrance to the palace. Maddī bade farewell to her parents-in-law, and taking leave of the other women and saying goodbye, she took her children and climbed into the carriage before Vessantara.

In explanation the Teacher said:

The princess Maddī, on whose every limb sat beauty, replied, 'Do not grieve, my lord, do not distress yourself. The children will fare just as we shall.'

With these words set off Maddī, on whose every limb sat beauty; with her children the lady blessed with beauty followed him along the Sivis' high road.

Then the nobly born king Vessantara, his great gift now given, 511
made a formal circumambulation of his parents and bade them farewell;

And mounting his carriage, a swift vehicle ready yoked with its four horses, he set out for Crooked Mountain with his wife and children.

In a place where a large crowd had gathered, King Vessantara said, 'We are going. May all my family be free from sickness!'

As the Great Being was starting on his journey, after he had exhorted the crowd never to neglect meritorious acts such as generous giving, the Bodhisatta's mother thought, 'My son, who is so splendid a giver, ought to give something now.' So she had sent to him on both sides carts filled with the seven kinds of jewels, as well as other trinkets. Vessantara took off the jewellery he wore on his own person too, and on eighteen occasions gave to those who came and asked, and so he gave away everything, without exception. When he had left the city he turned round, as he longed to take one more look, and because of his longing, the area of earth covered by his carriage detached itself and turned round, so that the carriage faced towards the city, and Vessantara could see his parents' home. And for that reason, there was an earthquake and other phenomena occurred.

So it is said:

[*Cp.*] When he turned round to gaze at the city he had left, then too the earth, wreathed by the woods of Sineru, quaked.

When he had gazed himself, he spoke this verse to make Maddī look:

> 'Look, Maddī, see this lovely sight: the home of the best of the Sivis, my father's house.'

512 When the Great Being had gazed on the sixty thousand councillors who had been born at the same time as he, and the rest of the people, he sent them back. As he drove the carriage he said to Maddī, 'My lady, look out for any suppliants who may follow us,' and so she sat watching. Now four brahmins who had been unable to arrive in time for the great gift of the seven hundreds had reached the city, and asked where the king was. When they heard that he had left after the gift-giving, they asked if he had taken anything with him when he left, and learning that he had gone in a carriage, they followed, intending to ask for the horses. Maddī saw them coming, and cried, 'Suppliants, my lord!' The Great Being stopped the carriage, and when they came up to him and asked for the horses, he gave them those four steeds.

a

b

9. (*a*) The steward tells Vessantara of his banishment. Degaldoruva (see C (*a*)).
(*b*) Vessantara breaks the news to Maddī, and they leave. Hanguranketa (see C (*b*)).

a

b

10. (*a*) Detail of 9 (*b*).

(*b*) Vessantara hears of his banishment, and Maddī asks to share it. Mural. Kumārakanda Maha Vihāra, Doḍanduva, Galle District. Mid nineteenth century?

a

b

11. (*a*) and (*b*). The gift of the seven hundreds. Kumārakanda (see 10 (*b*)). The story here reads from *R*. to *L*.; (*b*) is immediately under 10 (*b*).

a

b

12. (*a*) The gift of the seven hundreds. Kan̆dulova (see B).
(*b*) Same subject. Giddava (see D (*a*)).

13. *R.*: The Sivis complain to Sañjaya. *L.*: Vessantara bids farewell to Sañjaya and Maddī to Phusatī, who laments. Toṭagumuva (see 2).

14. Vessantara bids farewell to Sañjaya, Maddī and the children to Phusatī. Degaldoruva (see C (*a*)).

a

b

15. (*a*) Brahmins ask Vessantara for his horses. Bam̆baragala (see 7 (*b*)).

(*b*) *R. to L.*: Vessantara gives away horses; and carriage; and proceeds on foot with his family. Kumārakanda (see 10 (*b*)).

16. Vessantara gives away the carriage and they proceed on foot. Giddava (see D (*a*)).

In explanation the Teacher said:

> The brahmins followed him and asked for the horses, and at their request he gave the four steeds to the four of them.

When the horses were given away, the carriage's yoke-poles stayed where they were in mid air, and as soon as the brahmins had gone, four divine beings in the guise of red deer came, and by agreement moved off with the carriage. The Great Being, knowing they were divine beings, spoke this verse:

> 'Look, Maddī; see this wonderful sight: how our clever horses, looking like red deer, carry me on.'

But another brahmin approached him as he made his way, and asked for the carriage. So the Great Being lifted down his wife and children and gave the carriage to him. And when the carriage was given away, the divine beings disappeared. Explaining just how the carriage was given away, the Teacher said:

> A fifth approached him and asked for the carriage. At his request he gave it to him, and he was not cast down in spirit.
>
> Then King Vessantara lifted down his own family, and gratified the wealth-seeking brahmin with the gift of the carriage.

From then on they all went on foot; and the Great Being said 513
to Maddī,

[*Cp.*] 'You carry Kaṇhājinā, Maddī, for she is the younger and is light, and I will carry Jāli, her brother, as he is heavier.'

On his suggestion, then, they travelled each carrying a child on the hip.

In explanation the Teacher said:

> The king took the boy, the princess the little girl, and so they travelled in pleasant companionship, talking affectionately to one another.

End of the chapter about the Gift-giving.

WHEN they met some people travelling in the opposite direction, they asked, 'Where is Crooked Mountain?' and the people replied, 'It is a long way.'

So it is said:

[*Cp.*] Whenever anyone comes along our road going in the other direction, we ask them the way: 'Where is Crooked Mountain?'

[*Cp.*] When they see us there they show their sorrow, and give us painful news: 'Crooked Mountain is a long way off!'

The children cried out at the sight of the trees on either side of the road, heavy with all kinds of fruit. By the power of the Great Being the fruitful trees bent down to within the reach of his hands, and he picked out the ripest fruit and gave it to them. When Maddī saw this she spoke about the miracle.

So it is said:

[*Cp.*] When the children see the fruitful trees on the slope, they cry to have the fruit.

[*Cp.*] Seeing the children crying, the great trees in their distress bend down of themselves towards the children.

[*Cp.*] When Maddī, on whose every limb sat beauty, saw this marvellous sight, this thing so strange it would make your hair stand on end, she cried out her approval:

[*Cp.*] 'This is a marvel in this world, so strange it makes my hair stand on end. Because of the brilliant power of Vessantara, the very trees of themselves bend down low.'

514 Now from the city of Jetuttara to the mountain called Suvaṇṇagiritāla was a distance of five leagues; from there to the river Kontimārā was another five leagues; from there to the mountain Ārañjaragiri was another five; from there to the brahmin village of Foulstead [Dunniviṭṭha] was yet another five, and from there to his uncle's city was ten leagues; and so the journey from the city of Jetuttara was thirty leagues. Spirits, however, shortened the road, so that they took only one day to reach his uncle's city.

So it is said:

[*Cp.*] Out of pity for the children, spirits shortened the road; so that they reached the kingdom of the Cetans on the same day as they set out.

They set out on their journey from the city of Jetuttara at breakfast time, and reached his uncle's city in the kingdom of the Cetans in the evening.

In explanation the Teacher said:

> At the end of a long journey they reached the kingdom of the Cetans; a wealthy, prosperous country, rich in meat, drink, and rice.

At that time there were sixty thousand nobles living in his uncle's city. The Great Being did not go inside the city, but sat in a shelter at the city gate, where Maddī washed the dirt from the Great Being's feet and massaged them. Then she thought, 'I will let them know Vessantara has come', so she left the shelter and stood on the road within sight of him. The women going in and out of the city saw her and gathered round.

In explanation the Teacher said:

> The Cetan women gathered round when they saw the lady, blessed with beauty, who had come; 'Look! this delicate lady is making her way on foot!
>
> 'The noble lady is used to travelling around in carriages or in a palanquin: but today Maddī goes into the jungle on foot.'

When the crowd saw that Maddī and Vessantara and their 515
children had come with no protector at all, they went to tell the king, and the sixty thousand nobles, weeping in their concern, came to Vessantara.

In explanation the Teacher said:

> At sight of him the Cetan chiefs approached in tears;
>
> 'We hope you are well, my lord; we hope you are in health, my lord. Is your father well and are the Sivis free from sickness?
>
> 'Where are your forces, great king? Where is your array of chariots? You have come a very long journey without horses or chariot. Have you come to this region because you were defeated by your enemies?'

Then the Great Being told those chiefs the reason for his coming there:

'I am well, sir; I am in health, sir. My father is well, and the Sivis are free from sickness.

'I gave away to some brahmins a colossal trumpeter with tusks like poles, experienced on all battlefields, the all-white best of elephants;

'The rutting crusher of our enemies; covered with its white blanket, tusked, white as Mount Kelāsa, with its chowrie,

'Its white umbrella, its cushion, its keeper, its attendants: a noble bearer, a royal mount.

'Because of that, the Sivis were angry with me, and my father's mind was distressed. The king banished me and I am going to Crooked Mountain. Do you know, sir, a place in the forest where we may live?'

The chiefs replied:

516 'Welcome, great king, and very welcome! You have come as lord of all there is here. Let us know what you want,

'Of vegetables, lotus sprouts, honey, meat, pure rice, raw and cooked; and eat it, great king, for you have come here as our guest.'

Vessantara said:

'I take what you give; this is complete hospitality. The king has banished me and I am going to Crooked Mountain. Do you know, sir, a place in the forest where we may live?'

The chiefs replied:

'Stay here, O lord of charioteers, in the kingdom of the Cetans, until the Cetans go to the king to beseech him, to win over the great king, the bringer of prosperity to the kingdom of the Sivis.

'Then the Cetans will gladly follow you, taking what is necessary, and form your retinue. Know this, noble one.'

The Great Being said:

'Please do not go to beseech the king, to win over the great king, for the king is not the power there.

'The Sivis are haughty, both army and townsfolk, and want to destroy the king because of me.'

The chiefs replied: 517

'If that is the situation in that kingdom, O bringer of prosperity to the kingdom, take over power here among the Cetans.

'This kingdom is wealthy and prosperous; the surrounding country is rich and extensive. Make up your mind to govern this kingdom, Your Majesty.'

Vessantara said:

'Hear me, O Cetans! It is not my wish or intention to govern this kingdom when I have been exiled from my own kingdom.

'The Sivis, both army and townsfolk, would be displeased if the Cetans were to anoint me as king, since I have been banished from that kingdom.

'There would be great dissension between you because of me, and strife with the Sivis. And I do not like war.

'There would be terrible strife and great conflict. Because of me, one man, many people would be hurt.

'I take what you give; this is complete hospitality. The king has banished me, and I am going to Crooked Mountain. Do you know, sir, a place in the forest where we may live?'

And so, although they besought him in many ways, the Great Being refused the kingship. But those chiefs paid him great honour, for as he did not wish to enter the city, they decorated that shelter and made for it a curtain of hemp, and prepared a large couch, and all of them took up positions around it as a guard. He stayed in the shelter under their protection for a day and a night, and early in the morning of the next day he breakfasted on various fine-flavoured foods and then, surrounded by the chiefs, he left the shelter. The sixty thousand nobles escorted him along the
road for fifteen leagues, as far as the edge of the forest, and 518

described the fifteen leagues of the road that lay ahead in this way:

'Truly we will tell you where the virtuous and the royal ascetics, who have offered in the sacred fire and whose minds are composed, dwell in peace.

'See, there is the rocky mountain, great king, called Gandhamādana, where you will live with your wife and children.'

With mournful faces and tear-filled eyes, the Cetans gave him instructions: 'Go straight on from here, great king, keeping your face to the north.

'And then, most honoured sir, you will see lovely Mount Vipula with its cool shade, densely covered by clumps of trees of many kinds.

'When you have passed it, most honoured sir, you will see a mountain torrent, a deep river called the River Ketumatī.

'Between accessible banks its copious waters are full of fish like the finny carp. Bathe and drink there, and let your children refresh themselves.

'Then you will see, most honoured sir, a lovely banyan tree, with fruit sweet as honey, growing on a pleasant crest, and giving cool shade.

'Then you will see, most honoured sir, the rocky Mount Nālika, its slopes thronged with flocks of birds of many kinds, and frequented by fauns.

'To the north-east of that is Lake Mucalinda with its covering of lotuses and white water-lilies.

'Like a lion looking for meat, which plunges into a thicket, [plunge into] the forest, dense like a cloud, green with grass, full of trees in flower and trees heavy with fruit.

'There, up in the trees flowering in their season, countless birds of many colours answer one another in song with their beautiful staccato chirpings.

'When you have passed the difficult terrain of the mountain, and the sources of the rivers, you will see a lotus pond surrounded by karañja and kakudha trees,

'Its copious waters between accessible banks thronged with

fish like the finny carp. It is regular and square, sweet and fragrant.

'Build a leaf-hut to the north-east of that, and when you have built it, busy yourselves with gathering food.'

When the chiefs had in this way described his journey of fifteen 519
leagues, they took leave of him; but to allay their fears that Vessantara might meet some danger if any enemy of his should seize the chance to harm him, they posted an experienced and careful Cetan at the edge of the forest with instructions to stop all those coming and going. Then they returned to their own city.

Vessantara with his wife and children reached Mount Gandhamādana and stayed there that day, and then, with their faces to the north, they passed by the foot of Mount Vipula and made a halt on the banks of the river Ketumatī. There, when they had eaten the meat and honey given them by a forester, and had given him a golden needle, they bathed and drank. Then, their cares put to rest, they crossed the river and rested a while at the foot of a banyan tree growing on the top of a mountain ridge, and ate of its fruit. Leaving there, they reached on their journey Mount Nāḷika, and going round it, arrived at its north-eastern spur by the shore of Lake Mucalinda. There they entered the dense forest by a footpath wide enough for only one at a time. Passing through that, they reached the square lotus pond, which lay east of the river sources and the difficult terrain of the mountains.

At that moment Sakka, the king of the gods, paid attention and realized what was happening. Thinking that as the Great Being had entered the Himālaya region he ought to have a place to live
in, he summoned Vissakamma and sent him off with instructions 520
to go and build a hermitage in a beautiful spot in a valley of Crooked Mountain, and then to return to him. Vissakamma went and built two leaf-huts, two covered walks, and places for night and for day. At the ends of the covered walks he made groves of plantain with various kinds of flowering shrub appear in this place and that. He provided all that a hermit needs, and wrote the

words, 'Let any who desire to be hermits take this.' After he had driven away the spirits and the wild animals and birds whose cries are frightening, he returned to his own dwelling.

When the Great Being saw the narrow path, he thought, 'This will be a place for hermits to live in.' Leaving Maddī and the children at the entrance to the hermitage, he entered it himself, and when he saw the writing he knew that Sakka had seen him. He opened the door to the leaf-hut and went in. There he laid down his sword and bow and took off his outer clothes; he put on the dress of a hermit and came out of the hut holding a hermit's staff. He walked up and down in the covered walk and then went up to his wife and children, as calm and composed as one who by himself has found Enlightenment. Maddī fell at the feet of the Great Being and wept; and then with him she entered the hermitage. She went to her own leaf-hut and put on her hermit's dress, and then they dressed the children as hermits' children. And so those four of noble birth found a home in that valley of Crooked Mountain.

Maddī asked a favour of the Great Being: 'My lord, you are not to go searching for fruit and berries. You keep the children and stay here, and I will fetch fruit and berries.' From then on she brought fruit and berries from the jungle and looked after the other three. Then the Bodhisatta asked her a favour: 'Maddī, from now on we are hermits, and a woman is a stain on a life of renunciation. In future do not come to me at an improper time.' Maddī consented.

Because of the power of the Great Being's friendly sympathy, even the animals for three leagues in every direction began to live in harmony with one another.

Queen Maddī would rise early in the morning and set out food and drink, and would bring water for rinsing their mouths and give them tooth-sticks. She would sweep the hermitage and then,
521 leaving the children with their father, would go into the jungle carrying a basket, a spade, and a hook. When she had filled her basket with wild roots and fruit and berries, she would return at evening and put the fruit in her leaf-hut. She would tell the children to bathe, and then those four of noble birth would

A. *Top tier* (*L. to R.*): the Cetan forester waylays Jūjaka; he feeds him; Jūjaka proceeds on his way; Jūjaka bides his time by the square lotus pond; Maddī lies sleeping with the children and has her dream; she says good-bye for the day to Vessantara and the children.

Middle tier (*R. to L.*): Maddī searches for roots and fruits; the nearby maze; Vessantara gives Jūjaka the children; Jūjaka leads them off; he spends the night up a tree while a deity tends the children below.

Bottom tier: Vessantara's triumphal procession home, including the magic white elephant.

Painting on cloth.
Arattana Raja Maha Vihāra, Nuwara Eliya District. Mid eighteenth century?

a

b

B. Mural in 'old' (abandoned) shrine. Kan̆dulova Mädiriya Vihāra, Kurunegala District. First half nineteenth century?

(*a*) Vessantara gives away the elephant.

(*b*) He gives away his horses.

a

b

C. (*a*) Vessantara gives away his horses. Mural. Degaldoruva Raja Maha Vihāra, Kandy District. A date between 1753 and 1786. For painters' names see Coomaraswamy, p. 168.

(*b*) Vessantara gives away his carriage, which has been drawn by red deer. Mural. Hanguranketa Raja Mahā Vihāra, Nuwara Eliya District. 1870.

a

b

D. (*a*) Maddī delayed by the wild beasts in the forest. Mural. Giddava Vihāra, Kandy District. 1906.

(*b*) Maddī laments the absence of her children. Tableau: free-standing figures before painted background. Galenbiňdunuväva Vihāra, Anuradhapura District. 1964. Artist from Southern Province.

sit at the door of the hut and eat the fruit and the berries. Afterwards Maddī would go into her own hut with the royal children. In this way they lived for seven months in that mountain dale.

End of the chapter about Entering the Forest.

At that time there was living in the brahmin village of Foulstead in the kingdom of the Kaliṅgas a brahmin called Jūjaka. He left a hundred kahāpaṇas he had gained by begging in the care of a certain brahmin family while he went off again in search of more money. As he was away a long time the family spent the money, and when pressed for it on his return, since they were unable to give back the kahāpaṇas, they gave him their daughter, whose name was Amittatāpanā [scourge of enemies]. Returning with her to the brahmin village of Foulstead in the kingdom of the Kaliṅgas he made his home there, and Amittatāpanā cared for him very well. When some young brahmins saw the excellence of her conduct they upbraided their own wives: 'She looks after that brahmin well, even though he is old. Why do you neglect us?' The wives determined to drive Amittatāpanā away from that village, and whenever they were together, as at the river fords, they abused her.

In explanation the Teacher said:

There was living among the Kaliṅgas a brahmin named Jūjaka, and he had a young wife called Amittatāpanā.

The other women who had gone to the ford to fetch water from the river abused her, ganging up in their excitement, and saying,

'An enemy is your mother, an enemy your father, who gave you to a worn-out old man although you are so young.

'Your family plotted no good for you in secret, to give you to a worn-out old man although you are so young.

'Your family plotted a hard task for you in secret, and gave you to a worn-out old man although you are so young.

'Your family plotted evil for you in secret, and gave you to a worn-out old man although you are so young.

'Your family plotted hardship for you in secret, and gave you to a worn-out old man although you are so young.

522 'You lead a hard life, being so young and living with a worn-out old man; death would be better than your life.

'Your father and mother obviously could not find another husband for you, although you are so pretty and so marvellous: they gave you to a worn-out old man, even though you are so young.

'You must have sacrificed wrongly on the ninth lunar day, or not made the fire-offering, since they have given you to a worn-out old man, although you are so young.

'You must have offended wandering ascetics, brahmins, virtuous and learned, aiming at a life of restraint, so that you have to live with a worn-out old man, although you are so young.

'There is no suffering in being bitten by a snake, no suffering in being pierced by a sword, but that is suffering, and bitter too, to look at a worn-out old husband.

'There is no fun with an old husband, no pleasure, no easy talk. His laughter is not pretty.

'When a young man and a young woman talk together in private, whatever sorrows lodge in the heart of any woman melt away.

'You are young and comely, desirable to men. Go and stay with your family. What pleasure will a worn-out old man give you?'

At their mockery she took her water-jar and made her way home in tears. When the brahmin asked why she was crying, she spoke this verse in explanation:

523 'I will not go to the river to fetch water for you, O brahmin. The women mock me because you are old, O brahmin.'

Jūjaka said:

'Do not do the job for me, do not fetch water for me. I will fetch the water. Do not be angry, my lady.'

The brahmin girl replied:

'I was not born in the sort of family to let you fetch the water. Listen to this, brahmin: I will not live in your house!

'If you do not bring me a slave, man or woman, be sure of this, brahmin, I will not live with you.'

Jūjaka said:

'I have no craft, no money or grain, brahmin girl. Where shall I get a slave, man or woman, for my lady? I will serve my lady; do not be angry, my lady.'

The brahmin girl said:

'Come now, and I will tell you what I have heard. King Vessantara is living on Crooked Mountain.

'Go to him and ask him for a slave-boy and a slave-girl, brahmin, and when you ask him, that nobleman will give you a boy and girl as slaves.'

Jūjaka said:

'I am old and weak. The road is long and hard. Do not be sad, my lady, do not be depressed. I myself will serve my lady. Do not be angry, my lady.'

The brahmin girl said: 524

'Like someone who is beaten without a fight, without even reaching the battle, that is what you are like, brahmin: beaten before you go.

'If you do not bring me a slave, man or woman, brahmin, let me tell you this, brahmin: I will not live in your house. I will make things unpleasant for you. You will be sorry.

'When you see me dressed up at festivals and holidays, enjoying myself with other men, you will be sorry.

'Because of your grief when you no longer see me, old man, your head will be much whiter even than the top of Crooked Mountain.'

In explanation the Teacher said:

> Then the brahmin, frightened and subject to the brahmin girl, distressed by his passion, said to his wife:
>
> 'Get ready some provisions for my journey, brahmin girl: cakes and sugar-cakes, well made honey-balls and barley food.
>
> 'I will bring both of that pair of children to be your slaves. They will serve you unweariedly night and day.'

She quickly got ready his provisions and let him know. He made firm all the weak places in the house, and mended the door; brought firewood from the forest and brought water in a pitcher, filling all the bowls and dishes. Then he took his ascetic's dress, and after warning her not to go out after dark, but to take especial care until he returned, he put on his sandals and hung his bag of provisions from his shoulder. Taking formal leave of her, off he went, his eyes streaming with tears.

In explanation the Teacher said:

> When he had said this the kinsman of Brahman put on his sandals, and after he had given her instructions, he took formal leave of his wife.
>
> So off went the brahmin, keeping his vow, his face wet with tears, to the prosperous city of the Sivis on his way to search for slaves.

When he reached the city, he asked the crowd which collected, 'Where is Vessantara?'

525 In explanation the Teacher said:

> When he arrived at that place, he said to those who were congregated there, 'Where is King Vessantara? Where might I see the nobleman?'
>
> The people who were congregated there replied: 'The nobleman was undone by too much giving to people like you, brahmin. He has been banished from his own kingdom and is now living on Crooked Mountain.
>
> 'The nobleman was undone by too much giving to people like you, brahmin. He has taken his wife and children and is now living on Crooked Mountain.'

'You ruined our king, and yet back you have come. Just you wait here!' and they ran after him with sticks and clods of earth in their hands; but by divine intervention he managed to get on to the road to Crooked Mountain.

In explanation the Teacher said:

Urged on by his wife, greedy for his pleasures, the brahmin endured hardship in the forest, the home of fierce wild beasts, the haunt of the rhinoceros and the leopard.

Taking his staff of vilva wood, his sacred fire and water-pot, he entered the great jungle where he had heard was the granter of desires.

Once he was within the great jungle wolves surrounded him. Crying out, he strayed far from the path, and was lost.

And then that brahmin, unrestrained in his lusting for enjoyment, lost himself on a side-track of Crooked Mountain, and spoke these verses:

Sitting up a tree, besieged by dogs, he spoke these verses: 526

'Who can tell me about royal Vessantara, a bull among men, the unconquered conqueror, who gives security in time of fear?

'Who can tell me about the great king Vessantara? He is like the earth, for he is a refuge for those in need, as the earth is for her creatures.

'He is like the ocean, for those in need go to him, as the rivers flow to the sea. Who can tell me about the great king Vessantara?

'He is like a lovely lake, with cool water that is good to drink, and beautiful fords, its surface dotted with lotuses and sprinkled with the pollen from their filaments. Who can tell me about the great king Vessantara?

'He is like a lovely fig tree growing by the road, welcoming the weary with its cool shade, and easing their fatigue. Who can tell me about the great king Vessantara?

'He is like a lovely banyan tree growing by the road, welcoming the weary with its cool shade, and easing their fatigue. Who can tell me about the great king Vessantara?

'He is like a lovely mango tree growing by the road, welcoming the weary with its cool shade, and easing their fatigue. Who can tell me about the great king Vessantara?

'He is like a lovely sal tree growing by the road, welcoming the weary with its cool shade, and easing their fatigue. Who can tell me about the great king Vessantara?

'He is like a lovely tree growing by the road, welcoming the weary with its cool shade, and easing their fatigue. Who can tell me about the great king Vessantara?

'Now I have entered this great forest, whoever can answer to my lament "I can tell you!" will bring me great joy.

'Now I have entered this great forest, whoever can answer to my lament "I can tell you!" with that one sentence will generate great merit.'

527 The Cetan who had been left as a guard was walking in the jungle, for he had taken to hunting, and heard his mournful cry. He thought, 'This brahmin is shouting to find out where Vessantara lives. His is no honourable errand; he is up to no good. He will ask for Maddī or for the children. I shall kill him right here!' He went up to him, and drawing his bow, he uttered the threat, 'Brahmin, I shall not let you live!'

In explanation the Teacher said:

A Cetan hunter walking in the jungle heard him. 'The nobleman was undone by too much giving to people like you, brahmin. He was banished from his own kingdom, and lives on Crooked Mountain.

'The nobleman was undone by too much giving to people like you, brahmin. He took his wife and children and lives on Crooked Mountain.

'You stupid man, you do wrong to come to this wilderness from his kingdom, looking for the prince, as a heron looks for a fish in water.

'And so on this very spot I will cut short your life, brahmin. I shall shoot this arrow, and it shall drink of your blood!

'I will cut off your head and cut out your heart with its

strings, and make a sacrifice to the birds of the wayside with your flesh, brahmin.

'After I have cut out your heart, brahmin, I will make an offering of your flesh and your fat and your head.

'That will be a fine sacrifice, a fine offering of your flesh, brahmin, and you will not take away the prince's wife and children!'

When he heard his words, the brahmin, faced with the threat of 528
death, lied and said:

'Listen to me, Cetan: a brahmin messenger is inviolable, so people do not kill a messenger. That is the traditional custom.

'The Sivis are all appeased; his father wishes to see him; his mother is weak and her eyes will soon lose their sight.

'Listen to me, Cetan: I have been sent by them as a messenger. I shall take the prince back. If you know where he is, tell me.'

Then the Cetan, happy at the thought that he had indeed come to fetch Vessantara, tied up and restrained the dogs, and making the brahmin climb down and sit among the branches, he spoke this verse:

'The messenger for one who is dear is also dear to me. I will give you ample food, and this jar of honey and thigh of venison. And I will tell you the region where the giver of desires lives in peace.'

End of the chapter about Jūjaka.

WHEN the Cetan had fed the brahmin, and given him as provisions for his journey a gourd of honey and a thigh of roast venison, he put him on his path, and raising his right hand described the region where the Great King was living:

'See there the rocky mountain, great brahmin, called Gandhamādana, where the king Vessantara lives in peace with his children,

'Looking like a brahmin with his matted hair and garment of animal skin, with his hook and sacrificial ladle, sleeping on the ground and reverencing the sacred fire.

'There you can see dark trees bearing many kinds of fruit, like lofty black mountains with their dusky peaks in the clouds.

'Dhava shrubs, horse-ear trees, acacias, sal trees, and trembling creepers sway in the wind like youths with their first drink inside them.

'Above and around the trees is heard a sort of chorus, as najjuha birds and cuckoos fly in a crowd from tree to tree.

529 'Thronging among the branches and foliage they call out to the passer-by, delighting the newcomer, giving pleasure to those who live there, where the king Vessantara lives in peace with his children.

'Looking like a brahmin with his matted hair and garment of animal skin, with his hook and sacrificial ladle, sleeping on the ground and reverencing the sacred fire.'

Then he described the hermitage in greater detail:

'There are mango trees, wood-apples, bread-fruit trees and sal trees, rose-apples, beleric, yellow and emblic myrobolan, sacred fig trees and jujubes,

'Lovely timbarukkhas, banyans, and kapitthanas. The honey-trees drip honey, and ripe figs hang low.

'One can pick for oneself and eat pārevatas and bhaveyyas and succulent grapes and pure honey.

'And there some mango trees are in bloom, others in bud; on some the fruit is ripe, and on others not yet ready, both kinds the colour of a frog.

'Beneath the trees there a man can pick up ripe mangoes, and both the ripe and unripe fruit is of a superb colour, taste, and fragrance.

'Indeed it seems to me a miraculous place, full of wonder, that has the splendour of the Nandana Grove, where the gods dwell.

'Palmyras and coconut-palms, studded with many-coloured flowers as the sky is studded with stars, stand like woven garlands in a dense grove of date-palms, showing above it like the tips of streamers.

a

b

c

17. Details from Arattana cloth painting—see A. The story goes from *L.* to *R.* (*b*) and (*c*) are consecutive.

(*a*) After Vessantara has given the carriage, another brahmin hails him, and he makes yet another gift (of his personal ornaments?). Apocryphal episode.

(*b*) A Cetan informs the Cetan king of Vessantara's arrival.

(*c*) Vessantara and his family decline to stay with the Cetans, and take their leave.

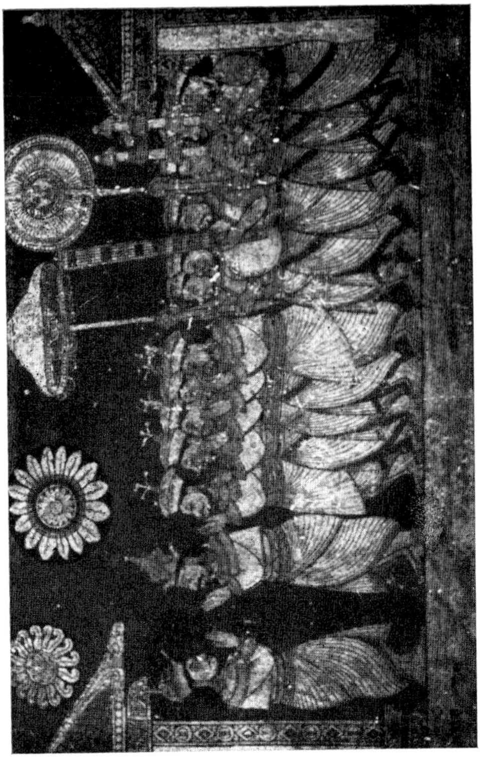

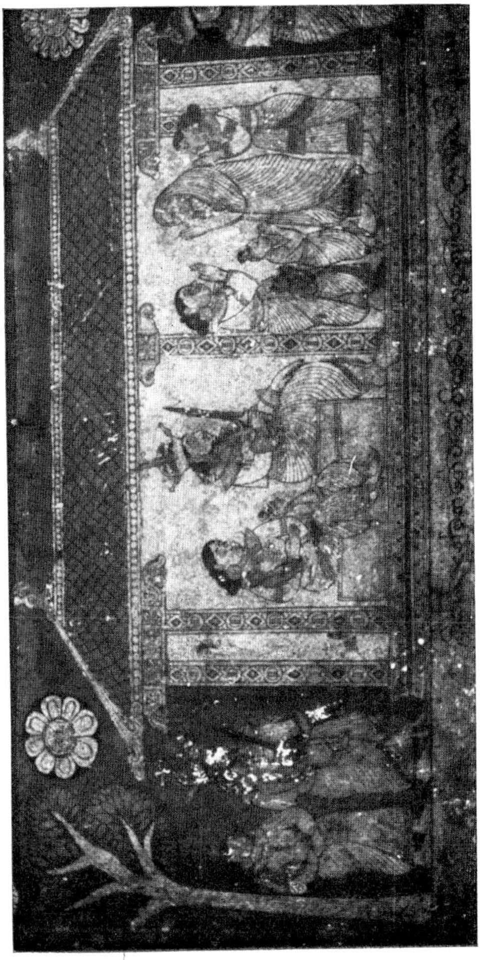

18, 19. Vessantara and his family arrive on foot and are greeted by the Cetans; he declines their offer of kingship, but takes his leave; they escort him to the edge of the forest. Consecutive scenes from Degaldoruva (see C (*a*)).

a

b

20. (*a*) Vessantara with the Cetans. Giddava (see D (*a*)).

(*b*) The Cetans see him off. Hanguranketa (see C (*b*)).

a

b

c

21. Details from Arattana cloth painting (see A). (*a*) and (*b*) go *R.* to *L.*

(*a*) Vessantara and family proceed after leaving the Cetans, and mountain spirits watch as they rest and feed the children.

(*b*) Someone points out the way to them (apocryphal episode: confusion with Accuta?); they are seen by the god Sakka.

(*c*) Maddī and the children in their own hut; they visit Vessantara in his; the almost obliter ated figure in the air on the *R.* must be Vissakamma.

a

b

22. (*a*) Maddī with the children in her hut; Vessantara looks after them while she (the damaged figure on the far *L.*) gathers food. Kan̆dulova (see B).

(*b*) After Vessantara has talked to his family, Maddī gathers food on Crooked Mountain (shown by the maze) and her hut stands empty. Mädavala (see Frontispiece). This scene adjoins the frontispiece on its *L.*

(*c*) Vessantara takes the children to his hut for the day. Degaldoruva (see C (*a*)).

c

a

b

23. (*a*) Amittatāpanā's parents cannot repay the money which Jūjaka deposited with them, so they give her to him in marriage, and he leads her off. Toṭagamuva (see 2).

(*b*) The women at the ford mock Amittatāpanā. Mural. Arattana Maha Vihāra (same temple as A). Second half nineteenth century?

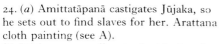

a

b

24. (*a*) Amittatāpanā castigates Jūjaka, so he sets out to find slaves for her. Arattana cloth painting (see A).
(*b*) Jūjaka says goodbye to Amittatāpanā. Mural. Sapugaskanda Maha Vihāra, Colombo District. *c*. 1950.
(*c*) Same subject. Giddava (see D (*a*)).

c

'There are kuṭajas, and kuṭṭha and tagara shrubs, blooming 530
trumpet flowers, punnāga trees and mountain punnāgas, flowering ebony,

'Uddāla trees, and somarukkhas, and many aloe trees, puttajīvas, and kakudhas, and flowering asanas.

'Kuṭaja roots, sweet-scented salaḷas, asoka trees, kosamba, bread-fruit and dhava shrubs, and sal trees are there, covered with flowers like a threshing floor with straw.

'Not far from there, in a spot as entrancing as the gods' Nandana Grove, is a lotus pond with a covering of white and blue lotuses.

'And there in the seasonably-flowering trees cuckoos, intoxicated with the liquor of the blooms, make the mountainside resound to their sweet singing.

'On each lotus leaf falls the sweet nectar of its flowers, and there the winds blow from the south and the west, so that the hermitage is sprinkled with the pollen from the lotus filaments.

'There grow strong water-plants, and two sorts of rice; there are fish and turtles gliding to and fro; and there are many crabs. And from the lotus fibres drips juice like honey, and from the lotus stalks juice like milk and ghee.

'A fragrant breeze moves in the forest, pervaded by many aromas, and steeps the forest with the scent of flowering branches.

'Bees are set buzzing all round by the scent of the flowers. And there are birds, many birds of all kinds of colours, singing out to one another, happily, with their mates.

'"Cheery children, deary children! Deary children! Cheer up, dearie!" [sing] the birds who live by the lotus pond.

'Like woven garlands [the trees] stand, looking like the tops of banners, fragrant with the perfume of the beautiful many-coloured flowers, there where the king Vessantara lives in peace with his children, looking like a brahmin with his matted hair and garment of animal skin, with his hook and sacrificial ladle, sleeping on the ground and reverencing the sacred fire.'

531 Jūjaka was pleased at the description which the Cetan gave him of Vessantara's home, and making a friendly response, he spoke this verse:

'I will give you this barley-meal cake of mine, bound together with honey, and well made honey-balls and barley food.'

At this the Cetan said:

'Keep the food for yourself; I do not want provisions. Take from here too, brahmin. Off you go, brahmin, at your ease.

532 'Here is a narrow footpath, which leads straight to the hermitage where lives the seer Accuta, grey with dust, with dirt between his teeth,

'Looking like a brahmin with his matted hair and garment of animal skin, with his hook and sacrificial ladle, sleeping on the ground and reverencing the sacred fire. When you reach him, ask him, and he will tell you your road.'

When he had heard this the kinsman of Brahmā took formal leave of the Cetan and set off exultantly for the seer Accuta.

End of the Short Description of the Forest.

On his way the descendant of the Vedic seer Bharadvāja saw the seer Accuta, and seeing him, he greeted him politely.

'I hope you are well, sir; I hope you are in health, sir. I hope you can live by gathering food and that there are roots and fruit in plenty.

'I hope there are few gadflies and mosquitoes and creepy-crawlies. I hope you meet with no harm in this forest thronged with wild beasts.'

The ascetic answered:

'I am well, brahmin; I am in health, brahmin. I can live by gathering food, and there are roots and fruit in plenty.

'There are few gadflies and mosquitoes and creepy-crawlies, and I meet with no harm in the forest thronged with wild beasts.

'I have lived for very many years in this hermitage, and I have not known any unpleasant affliction to occur.

'Welcome, great brahmin, and very welcome. Come inside, sir, and wash your feet.

'Eat, brahmin, of the very best: of honey-like fruit, tindukas and piyālas, madhukas and kāsumāris.

'Here too is cool water brought from a mountain cavern. Drink from it, great brahmin, if you wish.'

Jūjaka said:

'I take what you give; this is complete hospitality. I have 533
come to see the son of Sañjaya, who was banished by the Sivis. If you know of him, tell me.'

The ascetic replied:

'Your honour has no laudable motive for going to see the prince of the Sivis. I think your honour desires the prince's devoted wife.

'I think you want Kaṇhājinā and Jāli as slaves. Or you have come to take the three, to take mother and children away from the jungle. He has no possessions, no wealth or grain, brahmin.'

To this Jūjaka answered:

'I am not angry with you, sir. I have not come to beg. It is a fine thing to see noble men; it is always a happiness to live near them.

'I have never seen the Sivi prince who was banished by the Sivis, so I have come to look on him. If you know of him, tell me.'

The other believed him, and promising directions, pressed him to stay there for another day. On the following day, when he had fed him with various fruits, he stretched out his hand to show him his road:

'See there, great brahmin, the rocky mountain called Gandhamādana, where the king Vessantara lives in peace with his children,

'Looking like a brahmin with his matted hair and garment of animal skin, with his hook and sacrificial ladle, sleeping on the ground and reverencing the sacred fire.

'There you can see dark trees bearing many kinds of fruit, like lofty black mountains with their dusky peaks in the clouds.

534 'Dhava shrubs, horse-ear trees, acacias, sal trees and trembling creepers sway in the wind like youths with their first drink inside them.

'Above and around the trees is heard a sort of chorus, as najjuha birds and cuckoos fly in a crowd from tree to tree.

'Thronging among the branches and foliage they call out to the passer-by, delighting the newcomer, giving pleasure to those who live there, where the king Vessantara lives with his children,

'Looking like a brahmin with his matted hair and garment of animal skin, with his hook and sacrificial ladle, sleeping on the ground and reverencing the sacred fire.

'Clusters of musk-rose are scattered in that lovely spot; the ground is green with grass. No dust rises up there.

'The grass, rich-coloured as a peacock's throat, soft as cotton to the touch, grows nowhere higher than four fingers' height. Mangoes, rose-apples, wood-apples and low ripe figs: that forest gives delight with food-yielding trees.

'There glides flowing water, pure and fragrant, the colour of lapis lazuli, thronged with schools of fish.

'Not far from there in a spot entrancing as the gods' Nandana Grove is a lotus pond with a covering of white and blue lotuses.

'There are three kinds of lotus in that pond, brahmin, variously coloured dark blue, white, and red.'

When he had described the square lotus pond, he went on to talk of the lake Mucalinda:

'There the lotuses seem like linen, and the lake called Mucalinda is covered with white water-lily plants.

'There seem to be blossoming lotuses without number, a carpet of blossom to knee height in winter and summer.

'A fragrant breeze blows bearing with it various flowers, and bees are set buzzing all around by the flowers' scent.

(*The section omitted here is translated in Appendix I.*)

'In that place are birds, many birds of all kinds of colours, all singing sweet songs around Lake Mucalinda. 539

'In that place are birds, those birds called cuckoos, singing out to one another happily, with their mates.

'In that place are birds, those birds called cuckoos, all singing sweet songs around Lake Mucalinda.

'The forest, the haunt of elephants and home of kadali deer, is thronged with eṇi deer, and has a covering of creepers of every kind.

'In that place there is abundant mustard seed, wild rice, and beans in plenty; rice ripened in uncultivated soil, and much sugar-cane.

'Here is a narrow footpath which leads straight to the hermitage. Reaching there a man knows no hunger, no thirst, no discontent, there where the king Vessantara lives in peace with his children,

'Looking like a brahmin with his hook and sacrificial ladle, with matted hair and garment of animal skin, sleeping on the ground and reverencing the sacred fire.'

When he had heard this, the kinsman of Brahmā made a formal 540
circumambulation of the seer, and elated in heart set off for where Vessantara was.

End of the Long Description of the Forest.

WHEN Jūjaka reached the square lotus pond by the path described to him by the ascetic Accuta, he thought, 'It is too late today, for Maddī will by now have returned from the jungle, and womenfolk are just a hindrance. I shall go to the hermitage tomorrow when she has gone into the jungle, beg the children from Vessantara, and be off with them before she comes back.' So he climbed a mountain ridge not far from there and lay down to sleep in a comfortable place.

During that night, at dawn, Maddī had a dream, and the dream was like this: A dark man wearing two saffron robes and with red garlands adorning his ears came threatening her with a weapon in his hand. He entered the leaf-hut, and grasping Maddī by the hair, dragged her out and threw her flat on the ground. Then, as she shrieked, he dug out her eyes, cut off her arms, and splitting her breast took her heart, dripping blood, and went off. She woke up, terrified, and thinking, 'I have had a nightmare. No one can interpret dreams for me like Vessantara. I shall ask him about it,'
541 she went to the leaf-hut of the Great Being and knocked at the door. The Great Being said, 'Who is it?' 'My lord, it is I, Maddī,' she replied. 'Why have you broken our agreement, my lady, and come at an improper time?' 'My lord, it is not improper desires which bring me here, but I have had a nightmare.' 'Well then, tell me about it, Maddī.' When she had told him, just as she had experienced it, the Great Being understood the dream, and knew that he would fulfil the Perfection of giving, and that a suppliant would on the next day come and beg his children from him. He decided to console Maddī and send her away. 'Your mind must have been agitated because you were lying uncomfortably, or because of something you had eaten, Maddī. Do not be frightened.'

So he deceivingly consoled her, and sent her away. In the morning, when she had done all her chores, she embraced her two children and kissed them on the head, and warned them to be careful, since she had had a bad dream that night. Then, leaving them in the charge of the Great Being, with the words, 'Take good care of the children, my lord', she took her basket and other implements, and went into the forest in search of roots and fruit, wiping away her tears.

Jūjaka, sure she would by then be gone, came down from the mountain ridge and set off for the hermitage along the narrow footpath. The Great Being came out of the leaf-hut and sat down on a stone slab, looking like a golden statue. There he sat, thinking, 'The suppliant will come now,' looking at the path by which he would come, like a drunkard eager for a drink, while his children played at his feet. As he watched the path he saw the brahmin coming, and almost visibly taking up the yoke of liberality, which had been laid aside for seven months, he cried, 'Come then, brahmin!' and with great happiness addressed Prince Jāli in this verse:

'Up now, Jāli; stand firm! I think I see a sight from the past. I think I see a brahmin, and joy floods over me.'

To this the boy replied:

'I too see a man who looks like a brahmin, daddy. He comes 542
like a suppliant, and he will be our guest.'

And then the boy paid him respect, and rising from his seat went to meet the brahmin and offered to take his baggage. When the brahmin saw him he thought, 'This must be Vessantara's son, the prince Jāli. I shall speak roughly to him straightaway.' So he snapped his fingers at him saying, 'Be off, be off!' Thinking that the brahmin was terribly rough, and wondering what was the matter, the boy looked at his body and saw the eighteen human deformities. The brahmin approached the Bodhisatta and greeted him:

'I hope you are well, sir; I hope you are in health, sir. I hope you can live by gathering food and that there are roots and fruit in plenty.

'I hope there are few gadflies and mosquitoes and creepy-crawlies. I hope you meet with no harm in this forest thronged with wild beasts.'

The Bodhisatta answered him in a friendly spirit:

'We are well, brahmin; we are in health, brahmin. We can live by gathering food and there are roots and fruit in plenty.

'There are few gadflies and mosquitoes and creepy-crawlies, and we meet with no harm in the forest thronged with wild beasts.

'We have lived a life of sorrow in the forest for seven months, and you are the first godlike brahmin with vilva stick and sacred fire and water-pot that we have seen.

'Welcome, great brahmin, and very welcome. Come inside, sir, and wash your feet.

'Eat, brahmin, of the very best: of honey-like fruit, tindukas and piyālas, madhukas and kāsumāris.

'Here too is cool water brought from a mountain cavern. Drink from it, great brahmin, if you wish.'

Realizing that the brahmin would not have come to the great jungle without having a purpose in view, the Great Being determined to ask him straightaway the reason for his coming, and so spoke this verse:

543 'For what reason, for what purpose have you come to the great jungle? Tell me what I ask you.'

Jūjaka answered:

'As a full river never runs dry, I have come to beg from you. I ask you to give me your children.'

When he heard this the Great Being was filled with happiness, and as if putting a purse of a thousand gold coins in an outstretched hand, he cried out, making the mountain resound,

'I give, I do not hesitate. Take them as their master, brahmin. The princess went off in the morning, and she will return from gathering food in the evening.

'Stay for one night and go in the morning, brahmin, when she will have washed them and anointed them with scent, and adorned them with garlands.

'Then when you go you will take them hung about with many kinds of flowers, anointed with every fragrance, and carrying a plentiful variety of roots and fruit.'

But Jūjaka replied:

544 'I do not wish to stay, I would rather go. There may be trouble for me. I am going, lord of charioteers.

'Women are not open-handed; they are trouble-makers. They know spells; they take everything the wrong way.

'You are resolved to give the gift, so do not let me meet

their mother. She would cause trouble. I am going, lord of charioteers.

'Call your children; do not let them see their mother. In that way the merit you gain by giving a gift with resolve is increased.

'Call your children; do not let them see their mother. It is by giving treasure to someone like me, O prince, that a man goes to heaven.'

Vessantara answered:

'If you do not wish to see my devoted wife, let their grandfather see Jāli and Kaṇhājinā.

'When he sees these children, sweetly chattering in their dear voices, he will be glad and pleased, and delighted to give you much money.'

But Jūjaka said:

'Listen to me, O prince. I am afraid of robbery. The king might have me beaten, or might sell me, or kill me. Deprived of both wealth and slaves I should be an object of contempt to my brahmin wife.'

Vessantara said: 545

'Full of joy and gladness when he sees the children, sweetly chattering in their dear voices, the great king of the Sivis, who causes his kingdom to prosper and who always does what is right, will give you much money.'

Jūjaka answered:

'I shall not do what you urge. I shall take the children as servants for my wife.'

When the children heard his rough words, they rushed behind the leaf-hut, and then ran away from there and hid in a clump of bushes. But imagining Jūjaka coming and dragging them out even from there, they ran trembling this way and that, unable to keep still in any one place. When they reached the square lotus pond, putting on their strong bark clothes they slipped into the water and stood there, covered by the water with a lotus leaf over their heads.

In explanation the Teacher said:

> When they heard the words of that cruel man, the children Jāli and Kaṇhājinā ran trembling this way and that.

As Jūjaka could not see the children, he said to the Bodhisatta in reproach, 'Vessantara, just now you agreed to give me the children, but when I said I would not go to the city of Jetuttara, but would take them as servants for my wife, you gave them a signal to run away, while you sit here, all innocent. You must be the biggest liar in the world.' The Great Being was shaken by this, and realized that they must have run off. 'Do not worry, brahmin,' he said, 'I will fetch the children.' He rose and went to the back
546 of the leaf-hut, and knowing they had entered the forest thicket, followed their footprints to the shore of the lotus pond. When he saw that these continued into the water he knew that they must have gone down into the pond and be standing there, so he called out, 'Jāli dear,' and spoke these two verses:

> 'Come, my dear son, fulfil my Perfection. Consecrate my heart; do what I say.
>
> 'Be a steady boat to carry me on the sea of becoming. I shall cross to the further shore of birth, and make the world with its gods cross also.'

'Jāli dear!' he called out. The boy heard his father's voice and thought, 'Let the brahmin do with me what he will; I will not argue with my father,' and raising his head and removing the lotus leaves, he climbed out of the water and fell at the Great Being's right foot, clutching him tightly by the ankle and sobbing. The Great Being asked him, 'Where is your sister, my son?' But the boy answered, 'When they are in danger, daddy, people look after themselves.' The Great Being realized that the children must have made a pact with each other, so calling out, 'Come, Kaṇhā, my precious!' he spoke these two verses:

> 'Come, my dear daughter, fulfil my Perfection. Consecrate my heart; do what I say.

'Be a steady boat to carry me on the sea of becoming. I shall cross to the further shore of birth, and deliver the world with its gods.'

And she too, thinking, 'I will not argue with my father,' climbed out as the boy had done and fell at the Great Being's left foot, clutching him tightly by the ankle and sobbing. Their tears fell on to the Great Being's feet, which were the colour of a lotus in bloom, and his tears fell onto their backs, which were like slabs of gold. Then the Great Being made them get up, and said to comfort them, 'Dear Jāli, do you not know that giving brings me gladness? Help me to realize my aspiration.' And like someone valuing oxen, he put a price on his children just as he stood there, with these instructions to his son: 'Dear Jāli, when you wish to
be free, you can gain your freedom by paying the brahmin one 547
thousand gold coins. Your sister, however, is very lovely, and if someone of low birth were able to buy her freedom by paying a certain amount to the brahmin, there would result a great difference of rank in the marriage. But since no one but a king can give one hundred of everything, when your sister wishes to be free, she can buy her freedom by giving to the brahmin one hundred of everything, that is, one hundred male slaves, one hundred female slaves, one hundred elephants, one hundred horses, one hundred bullocks, and one hundred gold coins.' So he put a price on his children and comforted them, and took them to the hermitage. There he took water in a pot, and calling the brahmin to him, he formed an aspiration for omniscience; and as he poured out the water he made the earth resound with the words, 'Omniscience is a hundred times, a thousand times, a hundred thousand times more precious to me than my son!' and so made the gift of his dear children to the brahmin.

In explanation the Teacher said:

Then he who brought prosperity to the kingdom of the Sivis gave the children Jāli and Kaṇhājinā as a gift to the brahmin.

Gladly he gave his son and daughter, the children Jāli and Kaṇhājinā, as the best of gifts to the brahmin.

Then there was a frightening thing, then there was something to make your hair stand on end, for when he gave away the children, the earth shook.

Then there was a frightening thing, then there was something to make your hair stand on end, when the prince, who brought prosperity to the Sivis' kingdom, raising his folded hands, gave those luckless children as a gift to the brahmin.

548 After he had given this gift, full of joy because he had given so good a gift, the Great Being stood still, watching his children. Jūjaka went into a forest thicket, and biting off a creeper, used it to bind together the boy's right hand and the girl's left hand. Beating him with the ends of the creeper, he went off with them.

In explanation the Teacher said:

Then that cruel brahmin bit off a creeper. With the creeper he bound their hands, with the creeper he thrashed them.

Then, holding a rope and a stick, the brahmin led them away, beating them while the Sivi prince looked on.

Where they were beaten the skin broke and blood flowed, and as they were beaten they pressed back to back. The brahmin tripped on an uneven piece of ground, and fell, and the stiff creeper slipped off the soft hands of the children. In tears they ran right back to the Great Being.

In explanation the Teacher said:

Then the children broke free from the brahmin, and ran off. With eyes full of tears the boy gazed at his father.

Trembling like a leaf on a holy fig tree, he made obeisance at his father's feet, and having made obeisance he spoke these words:

'Mummy is out, and you are giving us away, daddy. When we have seen our mummy, then give us away.

'Mummy is out, and you are giving us away, daddy. Do not give us away until mummy comes back. Then let this brahmin sell us or kill us as he will.

'He is splay-footed; his nails are filthy; his calves are rolls of fat. He has a long upper lip; he slavers and his teeth stick out. He has a broken nose.

'He is pot-bellied, hunch-backed, and cross-eyed. His beard is red and his hair is yellow, and he is covered with wrinkles and freckles.

'With his red eyes, with massive hands, bent and deformed, wearing an antelope skin, he is horrible, he is not human.

'Is it a man, or a ghoul who feeds on flesh and blood, who 549
has come from the village to the jungle to ask you for money, daddy? How can you just look on as we are taken off by an ogre?

'Your heart must be made of stone or strongly bound with iron, if you do not care that we have been tied up by a brahmin greedy for money, excessive and ferocious, who drives us along like cattle.

'Let Kaṇhā stay here anyway; she does not understand. She cries like a fawn who has strayed from the herd and longs for its mother's milk.'

But the Great Being made no reply to these words. The boy 550
then, grieving for his mother and father, said:

'This is not so painful—for a man can bear it—but that I will not see my mother again, that is much more painful.

'This is not so painful—for a man can bear it—but that I will not see my father again, that is much more painful.

'My poor mother will weep for a long time, when she cannot see her daughter, pretty Kaṇhājinā.

'My poor father will weep for a long time, when he cannot see his daughter, pretty Kaṇhājinā.

'My poor mother will weep for a long time in the hermitage when she cannot see her daughter, pretty Kaṇhājinā.

'My poor father will weep for a long time in the hermitage when he cannot see his daughter, pretty Kaṇhājinā.

'My poor mother will cry for a long time, at midnight, through the night. Her tears will run dry, like a river.

'My poor father will cry for a long time, at midnight, through the night. His tears will run dry, like a river.

'All these different trees, these rose-apples and vedisas and sinduvāras—these we leave today.

'All these different fruits, these figs and bread-fruits, banyans and kapitthanas—these we leave today.

'Here are gardens, here a river with cool water, where we used to play: these we leave today.

'All these different flowers growing up on the hill, which we used to wear—these we leave today.

'All these different fruits growing up on the hill, which we used to eat—these we leave today.

'These toy elephants and horses, and these oxen of ours, with which we used to play: these we leave today.'

551 As he mourned like this with his sister, Jūjaka came up and took them off, beating them.

In explanation the Teacher said:

As they were driven away, the children said to their father, 'Wish our mummy well, and may you be happy, daddy!

'If you give these toy elephants and horses and oxen of ours to mummy, she will console herself with them.

'When mummy sees these toy elephants and horses and oxen of ours, she will restrain her sorrow.'

Overpowering grief rose up in the Great Being for his children, and his heart grew hot. Trembling like a rutting elephant seized by a maned lion, or like the moon caught in the jaws of Eclipse, his feelings unable to bear it, he went into the leaf-hut with eyes full of tears, and wept bitterly.

In explanation the Teacher said:

Then Vessantara, prince of noble birth, having given that gift, went into the leaf-hut and wept bitterly.

These are the verses of the Great Being's lament:

'Where will the children cry today in hunger and thirst at evening, at bedtime: "Who will give us food?"

'Where will the children cry today in hunger and thirst at evening, at bedtime: "Mummy, we are hungry. Give us food."

552 'How will they manage to walk along the road, with no shoes, tired on their swollen feet? Who will hold their hands?

'How could he not be ashamed, beating those innocent children in front of my face? That brahmin is shameless!

'Who with any idea of shame would beat even one of my slaves, or some other servant, even the lowest?

'Yet he scolds and beats my dear children, now that I am out of sight, as helplessly restricted as a fish caught in a net.'

The Great Being, feeling in his affection for his children that the brahmin was treating them too cruelly, and unable to bear the grief, considered running after the brahmin and killing him, and so bringing back the children. But a second thought convinced him that this was impossible. 'For to wish to redeem a gift once offered, because the suffering of children is too painful, is not the way of good men.'

In explanation of this matter, there are these two verses of inner debate:

'No! with my bow and my sword girded on my left side, I shall bring back my children; for I suffer when they are struck.

'Certainly it is painful to me that my children are beaten. But who, knowing what is expected of good men, regrets a gift once it has been made?'

Jūjaka drove on the children, beating them. And the boy sobbed 553
this lament:

'Indeed men speak the truth when they say: "He who has not his own mother is as good as dead."

'Come, Kaṇhā, let us die, we have no reason for living. We have been given away by the prince of men to a brahmin greedy for money, excessive and ferocious, who drives us along like cattle.

'All these different trees, these rose-apples and vedisas and sinduvāras—these we leave, Kaṇhā.

'All these different fruits, these figs and bread-fruits, banyans, and kapitthanas—these we leave, Kaṇhā.

'Here are gardens, here a river with cool water, where we used to play: these we leave, Kaṇjā.

> 'All these different flowers growing up on the hill, which we used to wear—these we leave, Kaṇhā.
>
> 'All these different fruits growing up on the hill, which we used to eat—these we leave, Kaṇhā.
>
> 'These toy elephants and horses, and these oxen of ours, with which we used to play: these we leave, Kaṇhā.'

Then the brahmin stumbled on an uneven piece of ground and fell, and the strap slipped from the children's hands. Trembling like chickens who have been struck, they ran off with a single impulse back to their father.

In explanation the Teacher said:

> As they were led away, the children, Jāli and Kaṇhājinā, escaped from the brahmin and ran this way and that.

554 Jūjaka got up quickly, and spitting like the fire at the end of an aeon, the stick and creeper in his hand, he caught up with them, and shouting, 'You are too clever at getting away!' he bound their hands and led them off again.

In explanation the Teacher said:

> Then, holding a rope and a stick, the brahmin led them away, beating them, while the Sivi prince looked on.

As they were led away like this Kaṇhājinā turned round to look at her father and cried out to him.

In explanation the Teacher said:

> Then Kaṇhājinā called out to him, 'O daddy, this brahmin beats me with a switch, as though I were a slave who had been born in his house.
>
> 'This is not a real brahmin, daddy, for brahmins are good men. This is a ghoul, disguised as a brahmin, who is leading us away to eat us. How can you just watch as we are driven away by an ogre?'

At the sight of his little daughter going off sobbing and trembling, overpowering grief rose up in the Great Being, and his heart grew hot. His breath came from his mouth in gasps, for he could not

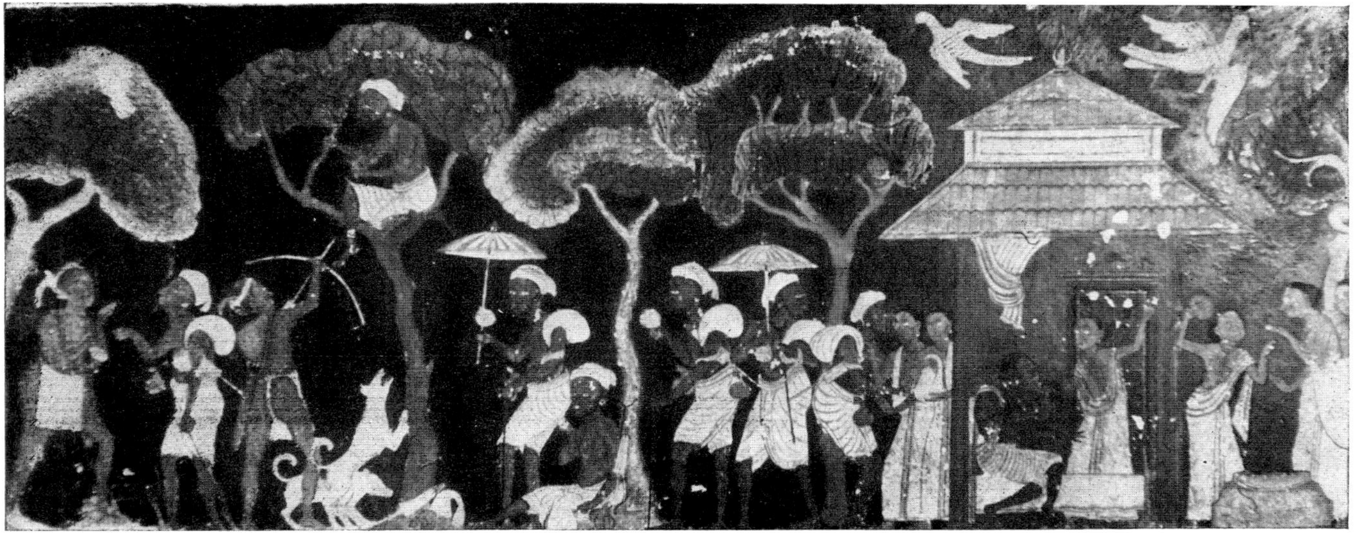

a

b

25. (*a*) *R. to L.*: Amittatāpanā at the well; she threatens Jūjaka; he says goodbye and sets off; he gets lost in the forest; the Cetan forester threatens to kill him; Jūjaka cajoles the forester. Käḷaṇiya (see 6 (*a*)).

(*b*) The Cetan threatens Jūjaka. Dehipāgoḍa (see 8).

26. The Cetan forester threatens to kill Jūjaka, and then feeds him; the seer Accuta directs Jūjaka on his way. Consecutive scenes from Degaldoruva (see C (*a*)).

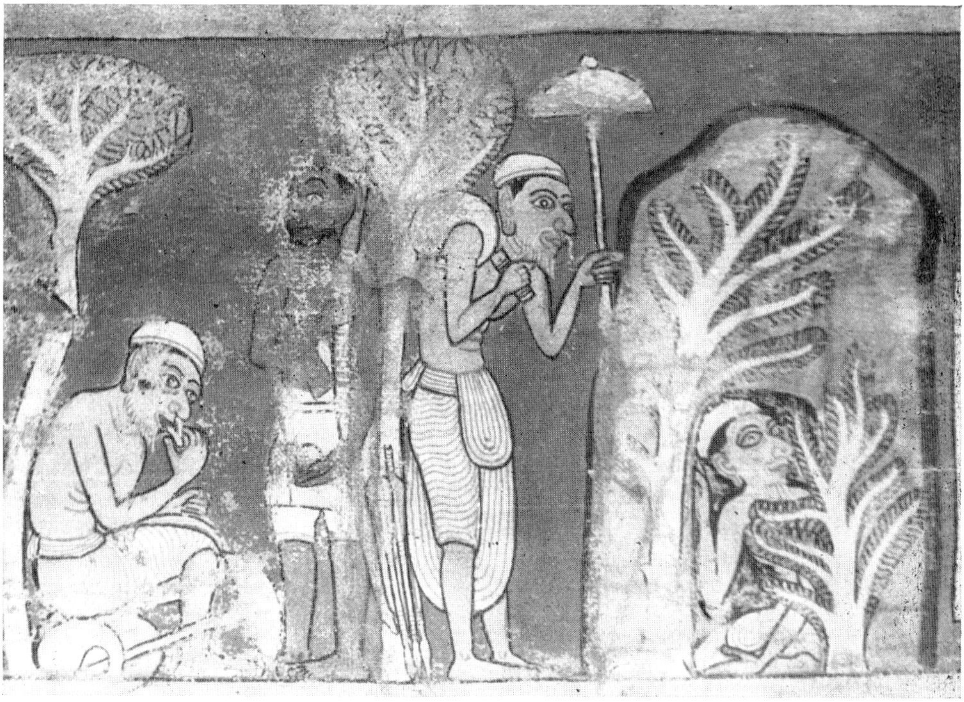

a

b

27. Details of Pl. A:
(*a*) The Cetan feeds Jūjaka. (*b*) Maddī's dream.

a

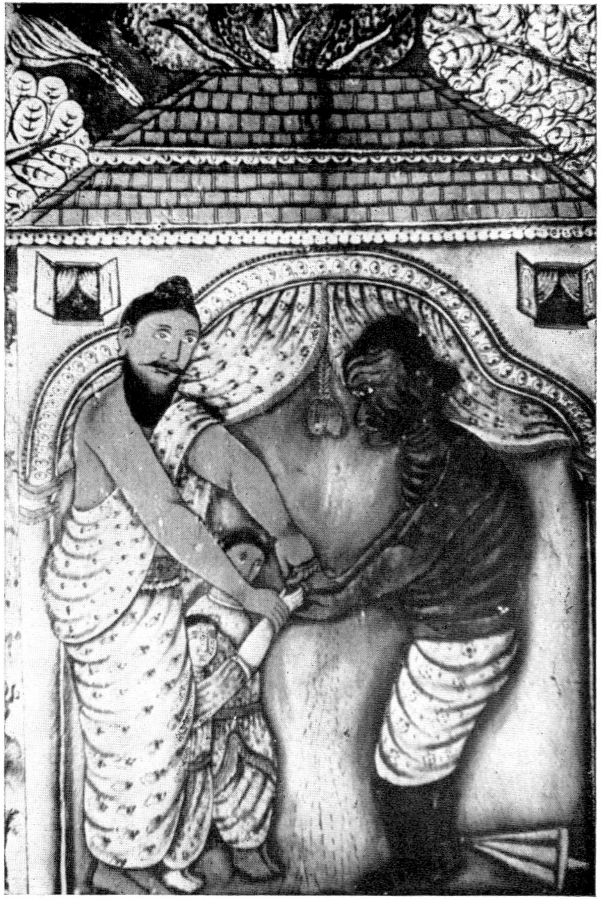

b

28. (*a*) Vessantara gives Jūjaka the children, but they hide in the lotus pond. Däḍigama (see 4).

(*b*) Vessantara gives away his children. Giddava (see D (*a*)).

a

b

29. (*a*) Vessantara gives Jūjaka the children, and he leads them off. Kaňdulova (see B).

(*b*) Vessantara gives Jūjaka the children while Maddī is away gathering food. Painting on cloth (*not* the same as A). Arattana Raja Maha Vihāra (see A). Second half eighteenth century?

30. (*a*) *Above*: Vessantara and Maddī in their separate huts. *Below*: a lion bars Maddī's way, while Sakka looks on. Mural. Veheragala Raja Maha Vihāra, Bihalpoḷa, Kurunegala District. Mid nineteenth century?

(*b*) Vessantara contemplates while Maddī swoons. Giddava (see D (*a*)).

a

b

a b

31. (*a*) Vessantara gives away Maddī. Mural. Gaḍalādeṇiya Raja Maha Vihāra, Kandy District. *c*. 1927.

(*b*) Same subject. Däḍigama (see 4).

a

b

32. (*a*) Vessantara gives away his children, then Maddī. Mural on wood. Pañduvasnuvara Vihāra, Kurunegala District. Early twentieth century.

(*b*) Vessantara gives Maddī to an old brahmin, who then turns out to be Sakka. Toṭagamuva (see 2).

breathe through his nose, and tears that were drops of blood poured from his eyes. Realizing that such pain overcame him because of a flaw in him, his affection, and for no other reason, and certain that that affection must be banished and equanimity developed, he plucked out that dart of grief by the power of his knowledge, and sat down in his usual position.

The girl sobbed aloud as she walked, before they even reached the mountain pass:

'Our feet hurt, the path is long and hard; the sun hangs so low, and the brahmin hurries us on.

'We cry out to the spirits of the mountains and of the forest; 555
we salute with bowed head the spirits of the lake and the accessible rivers.

'Grass and creepers, plants, mountains, and woods, please wish our mummy well. This brahmin is taking us away.

'Please, sirs, tell our mummy, our mother Maddī, "If you want to catch us up, you must follow us quickly.

'"This narrow path leads straight to the hermitage. If you follow it you will see us easily."

'Alas, when you bring fruit and roots from the forest, and see the hermitage empty, lady ascetic, you will be so sad.

'Gathering a lot of food is surely making mummy late, and she does not know that we have been tied up by a brahmin who is greedy for money, excessive and ferocious, who drives us along like cattle.

'If only we could see mummy today, back from her gathering in the evening, mummy would give the brahmin fruit mixed with honey.

'Then, satisfied after his meal, he would not make us hurry so much. Our feet are swollen, the brahmin makes us hurry so much.'

In this way, fretting for their mother, the children wept.

End of the section about the Children.

WHEN the prince made the earth roar by his gift of his precious 556
children to the brahmin, the uproar reached as high as Brahmā's

heaven. And those spirits who live on Mount Himavant, their hearts breaking at the sound of the grief-filled cries of the children as they were led off by the brahmin, said to one another: 'If Maddī gets back to the hermitage early, when she misses the children she will question Vessantara, and find out that they have been given away to the brahmin. Her love for them is so powerful that she will run after them, and so suffer great grief.' So they instructed some divine beings to obstruct Maddī's path in the guise of a lion, a tiger, and a leopard, and in spite of her entreaties, not to let her pass until sunset, so that she would reach the hermitage by moonlight. In this way they were to protect her from the harassment of lions and other wild beasts.

In explanation the Teacher said:

> Hearing their cries, three wild beasts of the forest, a lion, a tiger, and a leopard, spoke as follows:
>
> 'The princess must not return from gathering food this evening, but no wild animals in the forest, in our territory, must harass her.
>
> 'If a lion or a tiger or a leopard were to attack the lady blessed with beauty, Prince Jāli would be lost, and what would happen to Kaṇhājinā? The lady blessed with beauty would lose both her husband and her children.'

The divine beings agreed to carry out the instructions of those spirits, and taking the form of a lion, a tiger, and a leopard they went and lay down across the path by which she would come.

557 Maddī thought: 'Last night I had a nightmare, so I will gather roots and fruit and return to the hermitage in good time,' and trembling, she searched for roots and fruit. But her spade fell from her hand, her basket-strap slipped from her shoulder and her right eye throbbed; trees bearing fruit seemed bare, and bare trees seemed to be bearing fruit, and she completely lost her bearings. Thinking, 'What is happening today? It has never been like this before,' she said:

> 'My spade falls, my right eye throbs. Fruit-bearing trees are bare, and all the directions are confused for me.'

When she was returning to the hermitage in the evening when the sun had set, wild animals stood in her path.

'The sun hangs low in the sky, and the hermitage is far away. All they have to eat is the food I am bringing from here for them.

'The prince is waiting alone in his leaf-hut, trying to cheer up the hungry children when he does not see me coming.

'In the evening, at bedtime, my children will be like babies thirsty for milk. How wretched and miserable I am!

'In the evening, at bedtime, my children will be like people thirsting for water. How wretched and miserable I am!

'My children come out to meet me, like young calves running to their mother. How wretched and miserable I am!

'My children come out to meet me, like geese flying over a lake. How wretched and miserable I am!

'My children come out to meet me when I am near the hermitage. How wretched and miserable I am!

'There is only one way, one path, with the lake on one side and a pit on the other. I can see no other road which I might take to the hermitage.

'I pay you homage, O wild beasts, kings of great power in the wood. You are my brothers by Nature's law. I beg of you, let me pass on my way.

'I am the wife of that glorious prince who was exiled, and I shall never desert him, just as the devoted Sītā never deserted Rāma.

'You can see your children at evening, when it is time for sleep. I wish to see my children, Jāli and Kaṇhājinā.

'Here are roots and fruit in plenty, here is much to eat. I will give you half of it. I beg you, let me pass on my way.

'My mother is a princess, my father is a prince, so you are my 558
brothers by Nature's law. I beg you, let me pass.'

The divine beings considered, and realizing it was now time to let her pass on her way, they rose and went off.

In explanation the Teacher spoke this verse:

When they heard her pour out her gentle words filled with sadness, the animals moved from her path.

When the animals had gone, she carried on to the hermitage. Now it was the time of the full moon, but when she reached the end of the covered walk she could not see the children in the places where she usually saw them, and she said:

559 'This is the spot where the children usually come out to meet me, covered in dirt, like young calves running to their mother.

'This is the spot where the children usually come out to meet me, covered in dirt, like geese flying over a lake.

'This is the spot where the children usually come out to meet me, covered in dirt, not far from the hermitage.

'Like deer with their ears pricked up, they rush about in every direction, quivering, almost jumping in their joy and delight, but today I cannot see the children Jāli and Kaṇhājinā.

'Leaving the children behind, as a nanny-goat leaves her kids, like a bird freed from its cage I went out like a lioness searching for meat, but today I cannot see the children Jāli and Kaṇhājinā.

'Here are traces of them, like the tracks of elephants on a mountain: sand-castles dotted around near the hermitage. But today I cannot see the children Jāli and Kaṇhājinā.

'Covered with dirt, and dusted with sand, the children usually rush around here in all directions, but I cannot see my little ones.

'Always before they have come out to meet me as I returned from the distant jungle, but today I cannot see the children Jāli and Kaṇhājinā.

'Looking for me from far off they come out of the hermitage to meet me, like kids running to the nanny-goat, but I cannot see my little ones.

'Here is a yellow vilva fruit, a toy they have dropped, but today I cannot see the children Jāli and Kaṇhājinā.

'My breasts are full, my heart bursts. Today I cannot see the children Jāli and Kaṇhājinā.

'One sits on my lap, the girl clings to my breast, but today I cannot see the children Jāli and Kaṇhājinā.

'Covered in dirt at evening the children roll around in my lap, but I cannot see my little ones.

'Always before this hermitage has looked to me like a fair-ground, but today, when I cannot see my children, the hermitage seems to be spinning round.

'Why does the hermitage seem so quiet to me? Even the crows 560
are not cawing. My little ones must be dead!

'Why does the hermitage seem so quiet to me? Even the birds are not singing. My little ones must be dead!'

Mourning in this way she approached the Great Being and put down the basket of fruit. But when she saw him sitting so silently, and no children near him, she said:

'Why are you silent? I feel as if I am dreaming. Even the crows are not cawing. My little ones must have been killed!

'Why are you silent? I feel as if I am dreaming. Even the birds are not singing. My little ones must be dead!

'Perhaps wild beasts have eaten my children, noble lord. Or has someone carried them off into the jungle, the barren wilderness?

'Have you sent the sweet-voiced children off with a message, 561
or are they asleep? Or were they so intent on their games that they have wandered out?

'I cannot see the hair of Jāli's head, or his hands or feet. Did birds swoop down? Who has carried off my children?'

When the Great Being made no reply to her questions, she cried out, 'My lord, why will you not speak to me? What have I done wrong?

'This is worse pain. I feel a wound like the tearing of a dart, because today I do not see my children Jāli and Kaṇhājinā.

'This is a second dart which shatters my heart: today I do not see my children, and you will not speak to me.

'O prince, if tonight you do not explain to me, in the morning you will surely see me dead, all life gone.'

Thinking to stem her grief for her children by harsh words, the Great Being spoke this verse:

562 'Indeed, Maddī, famous princess of lovely hips, you went out this morning to gather food. Why have you returned so late this evening?'

So he said to her in feigned accusation, 'Maddī, you are beautiful and attractive, and in the Himālayan forests live a lot of people like ascetics and magicians. Who knows what you have been doing. You left early; why do you return so late? Married women do not behave like this, going off into the forest leaving young children. You did not so much as ask yourself what was happening to your children or what your husband would think, but left in the morning and are returning by moonlight. My unfortunate state is to blame for this.'

Hearing his words, she said:

'Surely you heard the noise of the lion roaring and the howl of the tiger who came to drink at the lake?

'There came a portent to me as I made my way through the great forest: my spade fell from my hand, and my basket-strap slipped from my shoulder.

'Then, trembling and afraid, I made many obeisances, and prayed to each direction that there might be safety from there.

'"Let not the prince be slain by a lion or a leopard. Let not the children be seized by bear or wolf or hyena."

'Three wild beasts, a lion, a tiger, and a leopard, besieged my path, and that is why I have come home so late.'

But having spoken only so much to her, the Great Being said nothing more before sunrise, and then Maddī poured out many lamentations:

563 'As a young disciple serves his teacher, so day and night I look after my husband and children, living the pure life of an ascetic with matted hair.

'Wearing the ascetic's antelope skin, bearing wild roots and fruit I make my journeys day and night because of my love for you, my children.

'I have brought for your play, my children, the golden turmeric, the yellow vilva fruit, the ripe fruits from the trees.

'O prince, eat with the children this lotus bulb and stalk, and these roots from the lily and water-plants, all mixed with honey.

'Give the red lotus to Jāli and the white to your daughter. Watch them dancing in their garlands. Call your children, O Sivi!

'Then, lord of charioteers, listen to the lovely sweet voice of Kaṇhājinā as she approaches the hermitage.

'We both, exiled from the kingdom, have shared the same joys and sorrows. Will you not show me the Sivi children, Jāli and Kaṇhājinā?

'I must have offended wandering ascetics somewhere in the world, brahmins, virtuous and learned men, aiming at a life of restraint, for today I cannot see my children, Jāli and Kaṇhājinā.'

The Great Being did not respond to her crying, and trembling 564
at his silence she went by the light of the moon in search of her children to the places where they used to play, among the rose-apples and the other trees, and there, weeping, she said:

'Here are all these different trees, the rose-apples and vedisas and sinduvāras, but there is no sight of the children.

'Here are all these different fruits, figs and bread-fruits, banyans and kapitthanas, but there is no sight of the children.

'Here are the gardens, here the river with cool water, where they used to play, but there is no sight of the children.

'Here are all these different flowers growing up on the hill, which they used to wear, but there is no sight of the children.

'Here are all these different fruits growing up on the hill, which they used to eat, but there is no sight of the children.

'Here are the toy elephants and horses, and these oxen of theirs, with which they used to play, but there is no sight of the children.

'Here are the dark hares and owls, and lots of antelopes, with which they used to play, but there is no sight of the children.

'Here are the swans and herons, and the peacocks with their many-coloured feathers, with which they used to play, but there is no sight of the children.'

When she could not see her precious children in the hermitage, she went out into the dense flowering forest, and looking now in one place, now in another, she cried:

'Here are the thickets which are always in flower, where they used to play, but there is no sight of the children.

'Here are the lovely lotus ponds, covered with mandālaka, lotus and palaka plants, echoing to the cries of the ruddy geese, where they used to play, but there is no sight of the children.'

565 As she could not see the children anywhere, she went back to the Great Being, and noticing how sad he looked, she said:

'You have not chopped the wood; you have not fetched water; you have not seen to the fire. Why are you brooding and doing nothing?

'When we who are dear to one another meet together, my weariness flies away; but today I do not see my children Jāli and Kaṇhājinā.'

The Great Being returned her words with silence. When he did not speak she was overcome by grief, and trembling like a hen which has been struck, she searched the places she had visited at first, and returning said:

'My lord, I cannot see where they are lying dead. Even the crows are not cawing. My little ones must have been killed.

'My lord, I cannot see where they are lying dead. Even the birds are not singing. My little ones must be dead.'

Even to these words the Great Being made no reply. In her grief for her children, thinking only of them, she hurried with the speed of the wind to the same places for the third time. All that night she searched the places they frequented to a distance of fifteen leagues. The night sky grew light, and as the sun rose she returned, and standing before the Great Being she sobbed.

In explanation the Teacher said:

When she had searched the hills and woods there she returned to the hermitage, and sobbed before her husband:

'My lord, I cannot see where they are lying dead. Even the 566
crows are not cawing. My little ones must have been killed.

'My lord, I cannot see where they are lying dead. Even the birds are not singing. My little ones must be dead.

'My lord, I cannot see where they are lying dead, though I searched among tree-roots and in the caves in the hills.'

So Maddī, the famous princess of lovely hips, stretched out her hands, gave a cry, and fell to the ground on that very spot.

Trembling at the thought that she was dead, the Great Being was filled with deep grief at the idea that Maddī had died in a remote and foreign place, since if she had died in the city of Jetuttara there would have been great ceremonial, and two kingdoms would have quaked. 'But I am alone in the forest,' he thought, 'What can I do?' Regaining his self-possession he rose to find out how she was. When he placed his hand on her heart he felt warmth, and so he brought water in a jar, and although he had not touched her body for seven months, the strength of his anxiety forced all consideration for his ascetic state from him, and with eyes filled with tears he raised her head and held it on his lap, and sprinkled her with the water. So he sat, stroking her face and her heart. After a little while Maddī regained consciousness and rose, and modestly she greeted him thus: 'Lord Vessantara, where have the children gone?' And he replied: 'My lady, I gave them as slaves to a brahmin.'

In explanation the Teacher said:

As the princess had fallen near him he sprinkled her with water when he saw that she was ill. Then he said this to her.

When Maddī asked him why he had not told her he had given 567
the children to a brahmin, but had let her wander around weeping all night, the Great Being replied:

'At first, Maddī, I did not wish to tell you the sad news.

A needy old brahmin came begging to our home, and I gave the children to him. Do not worry, Maddī; take comfort.

'Look to me, Maddī, not to the children. Do not grieve too much. We are alive and healthy. We shall have children.

'When a good man sees people who have come to beg, he would give his children or his cattle or grain or any other valuable goods that were in his house as a gift to them. Be glad with me, Maddī, for children are the very best gift.'

Maddī replied:

'I am glad for you, my lord; children are the very best gift. Now you have given them, let your mind be calm. Give more gifts.

'O king, among men who are full of greed you, the bringer of prosperity to the kingdom of the Sivis, gave a gift to a brahmin.'

To this the Great Being answered, 'Maddī, why do you say that? If my mind had not been calm after I gave away the children, these miracles would not have happened.' Then he told her about
568 the miracles, beginning with the roaring of the earth. Proclaiming the miracles, and rejoicing at the gift, Maddī cried out:

'The earth roared for you and the sound reached the three heavens. The lightning flashed on every side, and the mountains seemed to echo their agreement.

'Nārada and Pabbata rejoice at it with you; Inda and Brahmā and Pajāpati, Soma and King Vessavana and all of the thirty-three gods, together with Inda, rejoice.'

In this way the Great Being described his action, and Maddī expounded the matter, and saying, 'O great king Vessantara, the gift was indeed given well!' she praised the giving and sat down sharing his joy. Then the Teacher spoke the verse:

Thus Maddī, the famous princess of lovely hips, rejoiced with Vessantara, saying, 'Children are the very best gift.'

End of the section about Maddī.

As they talked together happily in this way, this thought occurred to Sakka: 'Yesterday King Vessantara made the earth roar by giving his children to Jūjaka, and today some low person may come and ask for the virtuous Maddī, who is blessed with every auspicious mark. He might go off with Maddī, leaving the king alone, helpless, and without support. I shall help him to reach the peak of Perfection by myself approaching him in the guise of a brahmin and asking for Maddī, so that she cannot be given away to anyone else. I shall then give her back to him and return here.' At sunrise therefore he went to him.

In explanation the Teacher said:

As night grew pale, early, towards sunrise, Sakka appeared to them in the guise of a brahmin.

'I hope you are well, sir. I hope you are in health, sir. I hope 569
you can live by gathering food, and that there are roots and fruit in plenty.

'I hope there are few gadflies and mosquitoes and creepy-crawlies. I hope you meet with no harm in this forest thronged with wild beasts.'

The Great Being answered:

'We are well, brahmin; we are in health, brahmin. We can live by gathering food, and there are roots and fruit in plenty.

'There are few gadflies or mosquitoes or creepy-crawlies, and we meet with no harm in the forest thronged with wild beasts.

'We have lived a life of sorrow in the jungle for seven months, and you are only the second godlike brahmin with vilva stick and cloak of antelope hide that we have seen.

'Welcome, great brahmin, and very welcome. Come inside, sir, and wash your feet.

'Eat, brahmin, of the very best: of honey-like fruit, of tindukas and piyālas, madhukas and kāsumāris.

'Here too is cool water brought from a mountain cavern. Drink from it, great brahmin, if you wish.'

When he had welcomed him kindly in this way, he asked him why he had come:

> 'For what reason, for what purpose have you come to the great jungle? Tell me what I ask you.'

Sakka answered, 'Great king, I am a very old man. I have come here to ask you for your wife Maddī. Give her to me.' Then he spoke this verse:

> 'As a full river never runs dry, I have come to beg from you. I ask you to give me your wife.'

When he heard this, the Great Being did not say, 'Yesterday I gave my children to a brahmin. How can I give Maddī away and be left alone in the jungle?' But, free from attachment and ties, his mind clinging to nothing, as if putting a purse containing a thousand gold coins in an outstretched hand, he spoke this verse, making the mountain resound:

> 570 'I give what you ask of me, brahmin, and I do not hesitate. I do not keep back what I have. My mind is glad at the gift.'

When he had said that, he quickly brought some water in a jar, and pouring the water over his hands, he gave his wife to the brahmin. All the miracles of the kind described before happened at that moment also.

In explanation the Teacher said:

> He who brought prosperity to the kingdom of the Sivis took the pot of water in one hand, and holding Maddī by the other, gave her as a gift to the brahmin.
>
> Then there was a frightening thing, then there was something to make your hair stand on end. When he gave up Maddī the earth quaked.
>
> Maddī did not frown at him; she felt no resentment or sorrow. Under his gaze she was silent, thinking, 'He knows what is best.'

'Look, brahmin, omniscience is a hundred, a thousand, a hundred thousand times dearer to me than Maddī. May this gift be the means for me to realize omniscience.' With these words he made the gift.

And this is said:

[*Cp.*] 'I was not afraid to give up Jāli and my daughter Kaṇhājinā, and my devoted wife the princess Maddī, for the sake of Enlightenment.

[*Cp.*] 'I am not indifferent to my children, nor to the princess Maddī. But Omniscience is precious to me, and for that I gave away even those people who were precious.'

Wondering how Maddī was feeling, the Great Being looked at her face. She asked why he looked at her, and like a lion roaring she spoke this verse:

'He whose virgin wife I became is my master and my lord. Let him give me away or sell me to whomever he wishes; let him kill me!'

When Sakka saw their noble intention, he spoke in their praise. 571
In explanation the Teacher said:

Knowing their resolve, the king of the gods said, 'All obstacles, both human and divine, have been overcome.

'The earth roared for you and the sound reached the three heavens. The lightning flashed on every side, and the mountains seemed to echo their agreement.

'Nārada and Pabbata rejoice at it with you; Inda and Brahmā and Pajāpati, Soma and King Vessavana and all the gods are glad, for he does what it is hard to do.

'Evil men do not imitate those who do what is hard to do, those who give what it is hard to give. The way of the good is hard to follow.

'For this reason good and evil men follow different courses after this life. The evil go to hell; the good end their journey in heaven.

'While you live in the forest you have given away your children and your wife. May that act bear fruit for you in heaven when you have taken the journey to Brahmā's realm.'

So Sakka expressed his sympathetic joy. Then, thinking, 'Now without delay I ought to give her back to him, and then go,' he said:

572 'My lord, I give you back your wife Maddī, on whose every limb sits beauty. You belong with Maddī, and Maddī belongs with her husband.

'Just as milk and a conch-shell are alike in colour, so you and Maddī are alike in heart and thoughts.

'You both, nobles of good lineage, of high birth on your mothers' and fathers' sides, were banished to the jungle here. Live in peace in a hermitage, so that you may do works of merit by giving again and again.'

After this he revealed himself in order to grant a wish:

'I who have come to you am Sakka, lord of the gods. Make a choice, O seer and king, for I will grant you eight wishes.'

Even as he spoke, by his divine powers he rose into the air, and stood there, blazing like the early morning sun. Making his choice, the Bodhisatta said:

'If, O Sakka, lord of beings, you have granted me a wish, this is the first wish I make: May my father be glad to see me returned from here to my own home. May he call me to take my seat.

'May I consent to no man's execution, even if he has committed a serious crime. May I free the condemned from death. This is the second wish I make.

'May the old, the young, and the middle-aged find in me support for life. This is the third wish I make.

'May I not go after another man's wife; may I be faithful to my own. May I not be dominated by women. This is the fourth wish I make.

'O Sakka, may a son be born to me and may he have a long life. May he conquer the earth with justice. This is the fifth wish I make.

'As the night grows pale, towards sunrise, may heavenly food appear. This is the sixth wish I make.

'May my bounty never cease. May I never regret a gift

I have made. By giving may I set my heart at peace. This is the seventh wish I make.

'When I am released from this life, may I go to heaven and 573
reach a higher state, and may I never be reborn from there. This is the eighth wish I make.'

When he heard his words the lord of the gods replied, 'Indeed before long your father will come to see you.'

Having encouraged the Great Being in this way, Sakka went off to his own dwelling.

In explanation the Teacher spoke this verse:

> When the king of the gods, Sujampati the Bountiful One, had said this, and had granted Vessantara his wishes, he went off to the heavenly assembly.

End of the section about Sakka.

So the Bodhisatta and Maddī lived happily together in the hermitage that had been given them by Sakka.

Meanwhile Jūjaka travelled sixty leagues with the children, and divine spirits looked after them. Each night at sunset Jūjaka tied the children to a bush, and made them lie down on the ground, while he himself, out of fear of fierce wild animals, climbed a tree and lay down in a fork of the branches. At that moment a spirit looking like Vessantara and a female spirit looking like Maddī would come and untie the children, and rub and wash their hands and feet, and restore their prettiness. They would give
them food to eat and a heavenly bed to sleep on, and at dawn 574
they would make them lie down just as they had been tied up, and then they would disappear. And so, with the help of these spirits, they went on their way without suffering. Also, because of divine prompting, Jūjaka decided to go to the kingdom of the Kaliṅgas, and reached the city of Jetuttara in a fortnight.

That day, just before dawn, Sañjaya the king of the Sivis had a dream, and his dream was like this: While he, the king, was sitting in the Great Hall of Judgement, a man brought two lotuses and placed them in his hand. The king fixed them to his ears, and their pollen drifted down on to his lap. When he woke in the morning he asked brahmins what it meant, and they explained that relatives of his who had been away a long time would return. That morning, when he had eaten foods of very fine flavours, he sat in the Hall of Judgement. The spirits led the brahmin there and placed him in the royal courtyard. At that moment the king looked round, and seeing the children he asked:

'Whose is that face which shines like gold refined in fire, like a golden coin beaten in the furnace?

'Their bodies, their features are alike. One is like Jāli, the other is like Kaṇhājinā.

'They are both alike, like a pair of lions coming out of a cave. These children seem to be made of gold.'

When he had described the children in these three verses, the king ordered one of his ministers to go and fetch the brahmin with the children. He hurried off and brought them, and the king said to the brahmin:

'O descendant of Bharadvāja, from where have you brought these children?'

Jūjaka replied:

'My lord Sañjaya, the man who gave the children to me was content; these little ones were given to me a fortnight ago.'

575 The king asked:

'As a fee for officiating at what sacrifice? I do not believe you received them lawfully. Who gave you this gift? Children are the very best gift.'

Jūjaka said:

'He who was a refuge for those in need, as the earth is for its creatures: it was the prince Vessantara who gave me the children, while he was living in the forest.

'Those in need would go to him as the rivers flow to the sea, and it was he, the prince Vessantara, who gave me the children while he was living in the forest.'

a

b

33. Mädavala (see Frontispiece). These two photographs, which overlap, constitute the *R*. half of the Mädavala cycle; the frontispiece is to their immediate *L*.

(*a*) Jūjaka leads off the children; he spends the night up a tree; he meets Sañjaya's steward.

(*b*) The steward reports to Sañjaya, who redeems the children, and Jūjaka eats, watched by a deity.

34. Same subjects as Plate 33. Mural. Daṁbadeṇiya Raja Maha Vihāra, Kurunegala District. Mid nineteenth century?

a

b

35. (*a*) Jūjaka up the tree; the steward informs Sañjaya, who redeems the children. Kaňdulova (see B).

(*b*) Jūjaka eating at Sañjaya's court. Dehipāgoḍa (see 8).

a

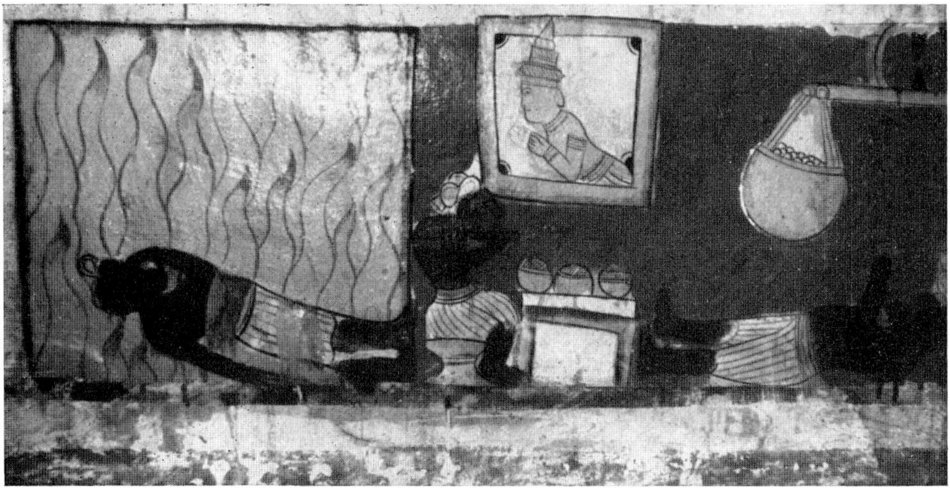

b

c

36. (*a*) Jūjaka eats till he dies. Däḍigama (see 4).

(*b*) Jūjaka eats, watched by a deity, till he falls into hell. Arattana mural (see 23 (*b*)).

(*c*) Jūjaka's death is announced by the public drummer. Mural. Pasgama Raja Maha Vihāra, Kandy District. Early twentieth century.

a

b

c

37. (*a*) Sañjaya orders his general to assemble the army. Arattana cloth painting (see A).

(*b*) and (*c*) The triumphal procession home. Daṁbadeṇiya (see 34). The photographs overlap.

a

b

38. (*a*) Vessantara gives away his children. Print by Sarlis. Early twentieth century. (*b*) Same scene. Popular print. *c.* 1950.

a

39. (*a*) Vessantara gives away his children. Postage stamp, after Degaldoruva. 1973. Actual size.

(*b*) Vessantara gives away the elephant. Mass produced batik hanging. 1974? Photographed in the Nātha Dēvālē, Kandy.

b

a

b

40. (*a*) Vessantara gives away his children. Cover of book—the play by John de Silva. Undated; 1960s.

(*b*) Same scene. Leaflet cover by G. S. Fernando. 1965.

When they heard this the ministers criticized Vessantara, saying,

'It would be wrong for the king to do this if he were living trustingly in his own home. How could he give away his children when he had been banished to the jungle?

'Take note of this, sirs, all you who have gathered here: how the prince Vessantara gave away his children while he was living in the forest.

'One could understand his giving away a male or a female slave, giving away a horse or an ass-cart, or giving away a trumpeting elephant; but how could he give away his children?'

The boy could not bear to hear this criticism of his father, and as though raising his arm on behalf of Mount Sineru buffeted by the wind, he spoke this verse:

'When a man has in his house no slave, no horse or ass-cart, no trumpeting elephant with long trunk, what can he give, grandfather?'

The king answered:

'I approve of his gift and do not blame him, my children. 576
When he gave you to the beggar, how did he feel in his heart?'

The boy said:

'His heart felt pain and his breath came hot. From my father's eyes, red as Rohiṇī, tears streamed down.'

Then he described what had been said:

'This is what Kaṇhājinā said: "O daddy, this brahmin beats me with a switch, as though I were a slave who had been born in his house.

'This is not a real brahmin, daddy, for brahmins are good men. This is a ghoul, disguised as a brahmin, who is leading us away to eat us. How can you just watch as we are driven away by an ogre?" '

When he saw that the brahmin made no move to free the children, the king spoke this verse:

> 'Your mother is a princess, your father is a prince. You used to climb on to my lap. Why do you stand so far away now?'

The boy replied:

> 'Our mother is a princess, our father is a prince, but we are slaves to this brahmin, and that is why we stand so far away.'

The king said:

> 'Do not say that, my dears, for it makes my heart burn as though my body were a funeral pyre, and I cannot be comfortable on my seat.
>
> 'Do not say that, my dears, and increase my sorrow. We shall redeem your freedom with a worthy gift, and you will no longer be slaves.
>
> 577 'When your father gave you to the brahmin, my dear boy, what price did he set on you? Tell me the truth, and then the brahmin can be paid.'

The boy replied:

> 'My father gave me to the brahmin at a price of a thousand gold coins, grandad, and gave his daughter Kaṇhājinā at the price of an elephant and a hundred.'

Ordering the children's ransom to be paid, the king said:

> 'Hurry, steward, and pay the brahmin. Give him as the children's ransom a hundred male and female slaves, a hundred cows, a hundred elephants, a hundred bulls, and a thousand gold coins.'
>
> Then the steward quickly paid off the brahmin, giving him as the children's ransom a hundred male and female slaves, a hundred cows, a hundred elephants, a hundred bulls, and a thousand gold coins.

He also gave the brahmin a seven-storied palace, and a large retinue. The brahmin gathered together his possessions and went up into his palace, where he feasted on fine food and lay down on a huge couch. Meanwhile the children were bathed, fed, and made pretty, and the grandfather and grandmother each took one of them on their laps.

In explanation the Teacher said:

When the children had been redeemed, and then bathed, fed, and adorned with ornaments, they took them on their laps.

When they had been washed from head to foot, and were 578
wearing clean clothes and all kinds of jewellery, the king their grandfather took them on to his lap and asked them questions.

When he had taken them, decked with tinkling earrings, garlands, and all kinds of adornments, on to his lap, the king spoke thus:

'I hope that both your mother and father are well, Jāli. I hope they can live by gathering food, and that there are roots and fruit in plenty.

'I hope there are few gadflies and mosquitoes and creepy-crawlies, and that they meet with no harm in the forest thronged with wild beasts.'

The boy replied:

'My mother and father are both well, Your Majesty. They can live by gathering food and there are roots and fruit in plenty.

'There are few gadflies and mosquitoes and creepy-crawlies, and they meet with no harm in the forest thronged with wild beasts.

'Through collecting the fruit of the trees in the wind and sun my mother has grown thin and pale like a delicate lotus which has been picked.

'Through her wanderings in the great wood, in the forest thronged with wild beasts, frequented by the rhinoceros and the leopard, my mother's hair has become thin.

'She digs up āluka and kalamba roots, biḷāli and takkala tubers; she gathers jujubes, marking-nuts and vilva fruits, and gives us them to eat.

'We do not eat during the day, but in the evening we eat all together whatever she brings when she comes carrying wild roots and fruit.

'She arranges her hair into the ascetic's matted plait, and with her armpits stained with sweat, wearing the garment of animal skin, she sleeps on the ground and reverences the sacred fire.'

After this description of his mother's pitiful state, he reproached his grandfather with this verse:

'Children are precious to people in this world, but for his children our grandfather can feel no affection.'

579 Then the king, confessing his own fault, said:

'I did a wicked thing, my dear child, like killing an unborn child, when I banished an innocent man at the command of the Sivis.

'Whatever I have here, whatever money or grain, let Vessantara come and govern as king in the realm of the Sivis.'

But the boy said:

'Your Majesty, the best of the Sivis will not come at my word alone. Your Majesty, go yourself and shower blessings on your own son.'

Then King Sañjaya gave instructions to his general: 'Let the army of infantry, chariots, horses and elephants be fitted out, and let the citizens and brahmin royal chaplains follow me.

'Let sixty thousand fine-looking fighting men quickly assemble, fully equipped and decked out in various colours,

'Some wearing blue, some dressed in yellow, some with red turbans, some wearing white. Let them quickly assemble, fully equipped and decked out in various uniforms.

'Just as that haunt of great crowds of animals, the snowy sweet-smelling peak of Gandhamādana, which is covered with many kinds of trees and with heavenly plants, spreads radiance and perfume to all the quarters, so let them, quickly assembled and fully equipped . . .[1]

[1] Half a line of the original is lost here.

'Then let men harness fourteen thousand elephants of independent will, with golden ribbons and golden trappings,

'Ridden by village headmen carrying pikes and goads. Let the mahouts quickly assemble, fully equipped, conspicuous on the elephants' backs.

'Then let men saddle fourteen thousand Sindh horses, thoroughbreds by birth, swift mounts,

'Ridden by village headmen carrying short-swords and bows. Let the riders quickly assemble, fully equipped and decked out on the horses' backs.

'Then let men yoke fourteen thousand chariots, with wheel- 580
rims expertly fashioned in iron and borders inlaid with gold.

'Let them raise the banners there, and put on leather and chain-mail. Let the strong-bowed archers draw their bows. Let the charioteers quickly assemble, fully equipped in their chariots.'

When the king had in this way given his plans for the army, he gave orders that the road his son would take, from the city of Jetuttara as far as Crooked Mountain, should be made even for a width of eight usabhas. Then he gave various directions for the decoration of the road:

'Let puffed rice be scattered and flowers, garlands, perfumes and ointments, and let gifts of hospitality be placed on the road he will travel.

'Let one hundred jars of toddy and spirits be placed by the wayside in each village on the road he will travel.

'Let meat and pancakes, cake and junket, together with fish, be placed by the wayside on the road he will travel.

'Let ghee and sesamum oil, curds and milk, panic seed, rice, and plenty of toddy be placed by the wayside on the road he will travel.

'Let there be chefs and cooks, dancers, mimes and singers, players of castanets, of jar-drums and bass-drums; and let there be comedians.

'Let them play all kinds of lutes, drums and kettle-drums. Let conches be blown; let the one-skinned drums sound out.

'Let them strike tabours and cymbals, play conches, and lutes with their resounding strings, and many other kinds of drums.'

581 In this way the king planned the decoration of the road. Jūjaka meanwhile ate too much, and not being able to digest it, died there and then. The king had his funeral rites performed, and had the drum beaten in the town, but when no relative of Jūjaka's appeared, his wealth reverted to the king.

A week later the whole army assembled, and taking Jāli as guide on the road, the king set off with that great following.

In explanation the Teacher said:

That was a great force, the zealous army of the Sivis, which set out for Crooked Mountain with Jāli as its guide on the road.

The sixty-year-old elephant of independent will trumpeted forth; while its harness was being tied on, the elephant trumpeted.

The thoroughbreds whinnied; the clatter of wheels began; the zealous army of the Sivis covered the sky with dust.

That was a great force, zealous and rapacious, which set off for Crooked Mountain with Jāli as its guide on the road.

They penetrated the great jungle, a mass of branches thronged with birds, crowded with trees in flower and trees in fruit.

There, up in the trees flowering in their season, birds of many colours answered one another in song with their beautiful staccato chirpings.

When they had completed a long journey, after several days and nights, they reached the region where Vessantara was.

582 End of the section about the Great King.

THE boy Jāli instructed them to pitch camp on the bank of Sumucalinda, and to position the fourteen thousand chariots facing the way they had come, and then he appointed guards in various spots against wild animals such as lions, tigers, and rhinoceroses. There was a great noise from the elephants and everything else. The Great Being heard it, and suspecting that his enemies had killed his father and had now come to deal with him, in fear for his life he took Maddī and climbed up the mountain, till he could look down on the army.

In explanation the Teacher said:

> Hearing the din they made Vessantara was afraid, and in fear he climbed up the mountainside and looked down on the army.
>
> 'Come here, Maddī, and hear what a din there is in the forest. Thoroughbreds whinny, and I can see the tops of banners.
>
> 'These must be hunters who will snare the herds of forest deer in nets, or trap them in pits, and with loud shouts will use their sharp weapons to kill all the best of them.
>
> 'We fell into the power of our enemies and were banished to the jungle although we had done nothing wrong. Witness now the slaughter of creatures powerless as we!'

Hearing his words she looked down at the army, and realizing it must be their own army, she spoke this verse to put heart into the Great Being:

> 'No enemy could overcome you, as fire cannot overcome 583
> a flood. Concentrate on that. In this there may be salvation.'

Then the Great Being shook off his despondency, and coming down from the mountain with her he sat down at the door of his leaf-hut.

In explanation the Teacher said:

> Then Prince Vessantara came down from the mountain and sat in his leaf-hut, with his mind made resolute.

At that moment Sañjaya called to the queen and said: 'My lady Phusatī, if we all go at once there will be too much weeping, so I shall go first, and when you think our excitement will be over, and we will be sitting peacefully, then you come with a large retinue. And after a short time Jāli and Kaṇhājinā may follow.' He had them turn round his chariot to face the way they had come, and set guards in various places, and then set off on the back of a richly caparisoned elephant to see his son.

In explanation the Teacher said:

When he had turned back the chariot, and posted his soldiers, the father went to his son who was living alone in the jungle.

Climbing down from the back of his elephant, with his robe over one shoulder, he made obeisance, and then, surrounded by his ministers, he approached to anoint his son.

There he saw the prince, who looked beautiful as he sat there in the leaf-hut, composed in concentration, free from any fear.

584 When they saw their father approaching with eagerness to see his son, Vessantara and Maddī went out to meet him, and greeted him.

Maddī paid respect to her father-in-law by bending her head to his feet, and said, 'I, Maddī, your daughter-in-law, bow at your feet in greeting, Your Majesty.' He embraced them there, and caressed them with his hand.

Then, when the king had cried and wept, and his sorrow was calmed, he said courteously:

'I hope you are well, my son; I hope you are in health, my son. I hope you can live by gathering food and that there are roots and fruit in plenty.

'I hope there are few gadflies and mosquitoes and creepy-crawlies. I hope you meet with no harm in the forest thronged with wild beasts.'

The Great Being replied to his father's words:

'We find a living, Your Majesty, such as it is, but living is hard for us. To live by gathering gleanings schools a needy man, Your Majesty, as a charioteer schools a horse. We are poor and we are tamed, for poverty has been our master.

'But our flesh has wasted away because we have missed seeing our mother and father, as we led our life of sorrow in exile in the jungle, O great king.'

After this he went on to ask for news of his children:

'They who were disappointed in the hope of being your heirs,

best of the Sivis, Jāli and Kaṇhājinā, are in the power of a brahmin, excessive and ferocious, who drives them like cattle.
'If you know anything of the royal children, tell us. Give us 585
relief quickly, as to a man bitten by a snake.'

The king replied:

'Both Jāli and Kaṇhājinā, your children, have been bought back. I gave the money to the brahmin, so do not worry, my son, but take comfort.'

When he heard this the Great Being was greatly relieved, and himself spoke words of courteous inquiry:

'I hope you are well, father; I hope you are in health, father. I hope, father, my mother's eyes are not worn out with weeping.'

The king replied:

'I am well, my son; I am in health, my son. And your mother's eyes are not worn out, my son.'

The Great Being asked:

'I hope your carriage is in good order; I hope your mount carries you well. I hope the country is prosperous, and that there is no lack of rainfall.'

The king answered:

'My carriage is in good order; my mount carries me well. The country is prosperous, and there is no lack of rainfall.'

While they were talking together in this way, Queen Phusatī decided that by then they would have assuaged their grief and be sitting peacefully, and so she made her way to her son with a large retinue.

In explanation the Teacher said: 586

While they were talking in this way, they saw their mother, the queen, at the mountain pass, walking barefoot.

When they saw their mother approaching with eagerness to see her son, Vessantara and Maddī went out to meet her, and greeted her.

> Maddī paid respect by bending her head to her mother-in-law's feet: 'I, Maddī, your daughter-in-law, bow at your feet in greeting, noble lady.'
>
> When the children, now safe and well, saw Maddī from far off, they cried out and ran to her like young calves to their mother.
>
> And when Maddī saw the children in the distance, and knew they were safe, quivering like the goddess of drink, she sprinkled them with streams of milk from her breasts.

She trembled, and with a loud cry fell senseless, and lay stretched on the ground. The children rushed up to her, and they too fell senseless on top of their mother. At that moment two streams of milk flowed from her breasts into their mouths, and if they had not received so much relief, the two children must have perished, their hearts parched. When Vessantara saw his precious children, he was unable to bear his emotion, and losing consciousness, he collapsed right there; and his mother and father also lost consciousness and collapsed on that very spot; and so did the sixty thousand ministers who had been born at the same time as Vessantara. Not one of those there could bear this piteous sight, and the whole hermitage was like a grove of sal-trees devastated by the storm at the end of an era.

At that moment the mountains roared, the earth quaked, the great ocean heaved, Sineru the king of mountains bowed low, and the six heavens of sensual pleasures were in tumult. Sakka the king of the gods, seeing that six nobles were lying unconscious, together with their retinue, and realizing that not one of them could stand up and sprinkle anyone else's body with water, decided to cause a lotus-leaf shower. So he caused a lotus-leaf shower to fall on the group of six nobles, and those who wished to be wet were made wet, while not a single drop stayed on those who did not wish to be wet. It was like a shower falling on a clump of lotuses, where the water seems to glide off the leaves. The
587 six nobles obtained relief, and the crowd cried, 'It is a miracle, for a lotus-leaf shower fell on the family, and the great earth quaked!'

In explanation the Teacher said:

When the family was reunited there was a great uproar. The mountains roared, and the great earth quaked.

The god made it rain, sending a shower at that very moment when the prince Vessantara came together with his family.

When the grandchildren, daughter-in-law, son, and king and queen were reunited, then there was a thing to make your hair stand on end.

All the people who had come out together from his kingdom made obeisance to Vessantara and Maddī in the terrible forest, and tearfully implored, 'You are our lord and king. May you both together govern our kingdom!'

End of the chapter about the Six Nobles.

WHEN he heard this the Great Being addressed this verse to his father:

'You and the country people and the townsfolk in assembly banished me from the kingdom, although I was governing the state in accordance with what is right.'

Asking pardon of his son, the king spoke this verse:

'I did a wicked thing, my son, like killing an unborn child, when I banished an innocent man at the command of the Sivis.'

Then, begging him to dispel his grief, he spoke this verse:

'One should destroy a father's grief in any form, or a mother's, or a sister's, even at the cost of one's own life.'

The Bodhisatta was willing to govern the kingdom, and even 588
before this had been said, he told the king that he had no objection. The Great Being accepted, saying, 'Very well,' and on realizing that he had agreed the sixty thousand ministers who had been born at the same time cried:

'It is the time for bathing, great king. Wash off the dust and sweat!'

The Great Being asked them to wait a little while, and going into the leaf-hut he took off his hermit's dress and prepared himself. Coming out of the hut he said, 'For nine and a half months I have lived the life of an ascetic here, and here the earth quaked when I attained the peak of Perfection by my giving.' Then when he had gone three times round the leaf-hut in respect, and had paid honour to it with the five-fold prostration, he stood before them. The barber trimmed his beard, and the other attendants completed his toilet, so that when they anointed him as ruler of the kingdom he shone in all his jewellery and adornments with the radiance of the king of the gods.

So it is said:

> Then King Vessantara washed off the dust and sweat.

Great splendour was his, and wherever he looked the ground shook. Those whose utterances were auspicious gave auspicious cries, and took up all sorts of musical instruments; and there was a noise like thunder in the depths of the great ocean. They decorated the finest elephant and led it up, and he bound on a fine sword and mounted that fine elephant, surrounded by the sixty thousand ministers who had been born at the same time, who wore every kind of ornament.

They also bathed Queen Maddī and adorned and anointed her, and as they sprinkled the water of consecration on her head, they cried out blessings, such as 'May Vessantara protect you!'

In explanation the Teacher said:

> When he was washed from head to foot and was wearing clean clothes and all kinds of jewellery, he mounted the proper elephant and bound on his sword, the scourge of his enemies.
>
> Then sixty thousand fine-looking fighting men of equal birth surrounded the lord of charioteers and made him glad.
>
> 589 And the Sivi maidens together bathed Maddī and cried, 'May Vessantara protect you, and Jāli and Kaṇhājinā; and may the great king Sañjaya watch over you!'
>
> For that reason, and because of their former misfortune, they celebrated in the lovely mountain glen.

For that reason, and because of their former misfortune, the lady blessed with beauty, reunited with her children, was full of joy and delight and happiness.

For that reason, and because of their former misfortune, the lady blessed with beauty was full of joy and delight and pleasure with her children.

Being so happy she said to her children:

'I had one meal a day and slept always on the stony ground, and that was the sacrifice I undertook because of my love for you, my children.

'Today that sacrifice is rewarded now I am reunited with you, my children. May that sacrifice undertaken by your mother and father protect you, my children.

Whatever works of merit your father and I have performed, by that truth, by that righteousness, may you be ageless and free from death.'

Queen Phusatī had boxes filled with dresses and jewellery for 590
her daughter-in-law to wear in the future, and sent them.

In explanation the Teacher said:

The mother-in-law sent to her daughter-in-law robes of cotton, silk, linen, and kodumbara cloth, which enhanced Maddī's beauty.

The mother-in-law sent to her daughter-in-law a golden necklace, a bracelet, and a jewelled girdle, which enhanced Maddī's beauty.

The mother-in-law sent to her daughter-in-law linen, a necklace, and a choker all of gems, which enhanced Maddī's beauty.

The mother-in-law sent to her daughter-in-law a tiara and a jewel for her brow, and gems of many colours, which enhanced Maddī's beauty.

The mother-in-law sent to her daughter-in-law trinkets, and a brooch, a girdle, and jewels for her feet, which enhanced Maddī's beauty.

As she looked at the jewels, both threaded and unthreaded,

that best of princesses shone with the radiance of a goddess in Nandana.

Washed from head to foot, and wearing clean clothes and all kinds of jewellery, the princess was as beautiful as a nymph in the heaven of the thirty-three gods.

Like a plantain tree stirred by the wind in a grove of many-coloured creepers, the princess with lovely lips shone in beauty.

Like a bird in woman's shape, with many-coloured plumage, the princess shone in beauty, her lips red as banyan or ripe bimba fruit.

591 They brought for her a trumpeting elephant who was not too old, a colossal beast with tusks like poles, unruffled by sword or arrow.

And Maddī mounted that trumpeter who was not too old, the colossal beast with tusks like poles, unruffled by sword or arrow.

And so they both made their way amid much pomp to the camp, where King Sañjaya organized mountain- and forest-sports for a month with twelve brigades. Because of the Great Being's influence no wild animal or bird in the great jungle harassed anyone.

In explanation the Teacher said:

Because of the power of Vessantara's character, none of the animals there in all the jungle harassed another.

Because of the power of Vessantara's character, none of the birds there in all the jungle harassed another.

Every animal there, throughout the whole jungle, gathered together in one place for the departure of Vessantara, the bringer of prosperity to the kingdom of the Sivis.

Every bird there, throughout the whole jungle, gathered together in one place for the departure of Vessantara, the bringer of prosperity to the kingdom of the Sivis.

Every animal there, throughout the whole jungle, stilled its pleasant noises at the departure of Vessantara, the bringer of prosperity to the kingdom of the Sivis.

Every bird there, throughout the whole jungle, stilled its

pleasant notes at the departure of Vessantara, the bringer of prosperity to the kingdom of the Sivis.

When the sports had been going on for a month, Sañjaya, the 592
lord of men, decided they had stayed in the jungle long enough, and summoned his army commander to ask him if the road his son would travel had been decorated. When the army commander informed him that it had, and that it was now time to go, he sent word to Vessantara, and then set off with his army. And so, in the midst of a large company, the Great Being travelled the sixty leagues of decorated road from the glen of Crooked Mountain to the city of Jetuttara.

In explanation the Teacher said:

The royal road to Jetuttara from where Vessantara lived was ready, decorated and strewn with flowers.

At the departure of Vessantara, the bringer of prosperity to the kingdom of the Sivis, sixty thousand fine-looking fighting men surrounded him on all sides.

At the departure of Vessantara, the bringer of prosperity to the kingdom of the Sivis, the women of the household, and the children, merchants and brahmins, surrounded him on all sides.

At the departure of Vessantara, the bringer of prosperity to the kingdom of the Sivis, the mahouts and guards, charioteers and foot-soldiers, surrounded him on all sides.

At the departure of Vessantara, the bringer of prosperity to the kingdom of the Sivis, well armed leather-clad soldiers in skull-helmets, with swords in their hands, went in front of him.

The king took two months to travel the road of sixty leagues, and reaching Jetuttara, he entered the city, which had been prepared and decked out for him, and went up to his palace.

In explanation the Teacher said:

They entered that lovely city, with its many archways and ramparts, now rich in food and drink, and full of dancing and singing.

The country people and townsfolk crowded together, full of

friendship towards the prince, when the bringer of prosperity to the kingdom of the Sivis arrived.

There was much waving of cloths at the coming of the giver of wealth. The drum announcing joyful tidings was sounded in the city, and an amnesty of prisoners was proclaimed.

593 The great king Vessantara had every creature set free, even the cats. Towards dawn on the very day he entered the city he thought, 'When the night sky grows light tomorrow suppliants will come, hearing that I have arrived. What shall I give them?' At that moment Sakka's throne grew hot, and noticing this, and knowing the reason for it, the god caused the seven jewels to shower down like a solid cloud, filling the ground to the east and west of the royal palace up to waist-height, and raining down on the whole city to knee-height. On the next day the Great Being had the treasure which had rained down in the grounds of various families to the east and west bestowed upon them. He had the rest collected, and putting it into his treasuries with the money from the grounds of his own house, he established largess.

In explanation the Teacher said:

At the entrance of Vessantara, the bringer of prosperity to the kingdom of the Sivis, the god made fall on that place a shower of gold.

The noble king Vessantara, after so much giving, at the dissolution of his body, full of wisdom, was reborn in heaven.

WHEN the Teacher had recited this exposition of the Teaching in this story of Vessantara adorned with a thousand verses, he gave the key to the jātaka.

'At that time Devadatta was Jūjaka and Ciñcamānavikā was Amittatāpanā. Channa was the Cetan, Sāriputta the ascetic Accuta, and Anuruddha was Sakka. The great king Suddhodana was Sañjaya, lord of men, and Mahāmāyā was Queen Phusatī. The mother of Rāhula was Queen Maddī, Rāhula was Prince Jāli, and Uppalavaṇṇā was Kaṇhājinā. The followers of the Buddha were the other attendants, and I myself was King Vessantara.'

End of the Story of Vessantara.

APPENDIX I

TRANSLATION OF 'THE LONG DESCRIPTION OF THE FOREST'

THE footnotes give, in the case of the flora named in the text, an identification which is generally accepted by various authorities, including the dictionaries, and is supported by similarities in the modern vernacular names. Where the only authority for an identification is the dictionary of the Pali Text Society, the letters P.T.S. precede the botanical name. The Sanskrit equivalent term, preceded by *Skt.*, is given when possible.

It was much more difficult to identify the animals and birds, and in their case the explanations of the commentator (indicated by the abbreviation Comm.) are provided.

ABBREVIATIONS used in the footnotes:

A *Indian Trees*, Dietrich Brandis, London, 1906.

B *An English Index to the Plants of India*, H. Piddington, Calcutta, 1832.

C *The Flowering Plants of Western India*, A. K. Nairne, London, 1894.

D *The Useful Plants of India*, H. Drury, London, 1873.

Hobson–Jobson *A Glossary of Colloquial Anglo-Indian Words . . .*, Yule and Burnell, London, 1903.

M–W *A Sanskrit–English Dictionary*, Sir M. Monier-Williams, Oxford, 1899.

AND in that place, brahmin, at the edge of the water stand trees; 535
kadambas[1] and trumpet-flower trees[2] in blossom, and flowering ebony,[3]
Aṃkolas,[4] kaccikāras[5] shrubs, and flowering pārijañña,[6] vāraṇa[7] and sāyana[8] trees, around Lake Mucalinda.

[1] kadamba: *Skt.* kadamba, *Anthocephalus Cadamba* (A, p. 367).

[2] pāṭalī: *Skt.* pāṭalī, *Stereospermum suaveolens* (A, p. 495).

[3] kovilāra: *Skt.* kovidāra, *Bauhinia purpurea* (A, p. 258).

[4] aṁkola: *Skt.* añkola, *Alangium Lamarckii* (A, p. 354).

[5] kaccikāra: P.T.S. *Caesalpina digyna* (A, p. 247).

[6] pārijañña: (P.T.S. = pārichattaka) ?*Skt.* pārijāta/pārijātaka, *Erythrina indica* (A, p. 226) or *Nyctanthes arbortristis* (A, p. 442; C, p. 176). Comm. 'katamāla': ?*Skt.* kṛtamāla, *Cassia Fistula* (A, p. 253).

[7] vāraṇa: *Skt.* varaṇa, *Crataeva Roxburghii* (A, p. 32).

[8] sāyana: Comm. '= nāgarukkha': *Skt.* nāgakesara, *Mesua ferrea* (A, p. 55).

Acacias,[1] white tulip-trees[2] and padmakas[3] diffuse their fragrance. And there are nigguṇḍi[4] and (black/lucky) nigguṇḍi[5] shrubs, and flowering asanas[6] in that place.

There paṅgura[7] and vakula[8] trees, sāl[9] and horse-radish[10] trees in flower, ketakas[11] and kaṇikāras[12] and kaṇaveras[13] in blossom,

Ajjuna[14] trees and ajjukaṇṇas[15] and blossoming oleanders[16] stand, and kiṁsukas,[17] their tops ablaze with full blooms.

The white-leaf tree,[18] the seven-leaf tree,[19] plantain[20] and safflower,[21] the bow acacia[22] in bloom, the siṁsapa[23] and varaṇa,

Acchivas[24] and sibala[25] trees, and incense-trees[26] in blossom, setagerus[27] and tagara[28] shrubs, maṁsi[29] plants, kuṭṭhas[30] and kulāvaras,[31]

Saplings and mature trees, straight and flowering, surround the hermitage on both sides, all around the hut with its fire.

536   And in that place at the edge of the water is marjoram[32] in abundance.

[1] sirīsa: *Skt.* śirīṣa, *Albizzia Lebbek* (A, pp. 271–2).

[2] setavārisa: *Skt.* pāriśa, *Thespesia populnea* (A, p. 75). Comm. '= setaccha-rukkha'; cf. v. 419 where Comm. 'these trees have white trunks, large leaves, and flowers similar to those of the kaṇikāra tree'.

[3] padmaka: *Skt.* padmaka, P.T.S. *Costus speciosus* (B, p. 24).

[4] nigguṇḍi: *Skt.* nirguṇḍī, *Vitex Negundo* (A, p. 503).

[5] sirinigguṇḍi: Comm. 'pakatinigguṇḍī c'eva kālanigguṇḍī ca', 'common nigguṇḍi and black nigguṇḍi'.

[6] asana: *Skt.* asana, *Terminalia tomentosa* (A, p. 310).

[7] paṅgura: identification impossible.

[8] vakula: *Skt.* vakula, *Mimusops Elengi* (A, p. 425).

[9] sāla: *Skt.* śāla/sāla, *Shorea robusta* (A, p. 71).

[10] sobhañjanaka: *Skt.* śobhāñjana, *Moringa pterygospermum* (A, p. 209).

[11] ketaka: *Skt.* ketaka, *Pandanus tectorius* or *odoratissimus* (A, p. 659).

[12] kaṇikāra: *Skt.* karṇikāra, *Pterospermum acerifolium* (A, p. 91).

[13] kaṇavera: *Skt.* karavīra, *Nerium odorum* (A, p. 462).

[14] ajjuna: *Skt.* arjuna, *Terminalia Arjuna* (A, p. 311).

[15] ajjukaṇṇa: P.T.S. *Pentaptera tomentosa*, possibly *Terminalia tomentosa* (A, p. 310).   [16] kaṇavera: *Skt.* karavīra, *Nerium odorum* (A, p. 462).

[17] kiṁsuka: *Skt.* kiṁsuka, *Butea frondosa* (A, p. 230).

[18] setapaṇṇi: possibly *Polygonum lanatum* (B, p. 71).

[19] sattapaṇṇa: *Skt.* saptaparṇa, *Alstonia scholaris* (A, p. 459).

[20] kadaliyo: *Skt.* kadalī, *Musa sapientum* (B, p. 58).

[21] kusumbhara: *Skt.* kusumbha, *Carthamus tinctorius* (B, p. 18).

[22] dhanutakkari: *Skt.* tarkārī, *Sesbania aegyptiaca* (A, p. 219).

[23] siṁsapa: *Skt.* śiṁśapa, *Dalbergia Sissoo* (A, p. 233).

[24] acchiva: *Skt.* akṣ⁽ī⁾ba, *Moringa pterygospermum* (A, p. 209).

[25] sibala: identification impossible.

[26] sallakiyo: *Skt.* śallakī, *Boswellia serrata* or *thurifera* (A, p. 129).

[27] setageru: identification impossible.

[28] tagara: *Skt.* tagara, *Tabernaemontana coronaria* (A, p. 460).

[29] maṁsi: *Skt.* māṁsī, *Valeriana Jatamansi* (B, p. 90).

[30] kuṭṭha: *Skt.* kuṣṭha, *Costus speciosus* (B, p. 245; cf. also Hobson–Jobson).

[31] kulāvara: identification impossible.

[32] phaṇijjaka: *Skt.* phaṇijjhaka, P.T.S. *Origanum vulgare*.

There are kidney beans[1] and karati beans,[2] water-herbs[3] and water-plants.[4]

Gadflies [hover] above waving assafoetida[5] buds; and there are dāsima[6] and kañcaka[7] plants, and much low convolvulus.[8]

Covered with creeping vines the trees stand, brahmin. [Their blossoms] can be carried for a week before their perfume fades.

On both sides of Lake Mucalinda with its covering of blue water-lilies grow lovely flowers, and the forest is made beautiful. They can be carried for a fortnight before their perfume fades.

There are blue-blossom plants,[9] and sekadhāris,[10] and mountain kaṇṇikas[11] in flower, and the forest has a covering of kaṭeruka[12] creepers and basil.

The forest is steeped with the scent of flowering branches, and bees are set buzzing all around by the flowers' fragrance.

By that lake, brahmin, there are three kinds of pumpkin.[13] The fruit of one is the size of a pot, the fruit of the other two is the size of a small drum.

And in that place there is mustard seed in abundance, growing in the water, tinged with green.[14] Asīs[15] stand like palm fans, and there are many blue water-lilies to be plucked.

Jasmine[16] and the sun-creeper,[17] dark and smelling like honey, the asoka[18] and mudayanti,[19] the gourd with its small flowers,

1 mugga(ti): *Skt.* mudga, *Phaseolus Mungo* (D, p. 337).

2 karati: Comm. '= rājamāsa', 'bean'. Other identification is impossible.

3 sevāla: *Skt.* śev(ā)la/śaiv(ā)la, *Vallisneria spiralis* (C, p. 317).

4 siṁsaka: Comm. '= rattacandana', 'red sandal'. Other identification is impossible.

5 hiṅgu: *Skt.* hiṅgu, *Ferula Assafoetida* (B, p. 37; C, p. 136).

6 dāsima: identification impossible.

7 kañcaka: possibly *Abrus precatorius*, vetch. (B, p. 1).

8 kalambaka: *Skt.* kalambī, *Convolvulus reptans* (B, p. 23).

9 nīlapupphi: *Skt.* nīlapuṣpi, *Clitoria ternatea* (B, p. 22; C, p. 89). Comm. 'nīlapupphīti ādikā pupphavalliyo'.

10 sekadhāri: identification impossible.

11 girikaṇṇika: *Skt.* girikarṇika, P.T.S. *Clitoria ternatea.*

12 kaṭeruka: perhaps = kaṭeruha: *Skt.* kaśeruka, *Scirpus Kysoor* (B, p. 80).

13 kakkāru: *Skt.* karkāru, *Cucurbita pepo* (B, p. 26; C, p. 130).

14 haritāyuto: Comm. 'haritena āyuto nādiyo ime dve lasunajātiyo' '... two kinds of garlic'.

15 asī: identification impossible.

16 apphoṭa: *Skt.* āsphota, *Jasminum Zambac* (B, p. 47).

17 suriyavallī: *Skt.* sūryavallī, *Croton plicatum* (B, p. 25) or, M-W, *Gynandropsis pentaphylla* (C, p. 16).

18 asoka: *Skt.* aśoka, *Jonesia Asoka* (B, p. 48).

19 mudayanti: ?*Skt.* modayanti, *Ligusticum diffusum* or *Ajowan* (B, p. 51).

Koraṇḍaka[1] and flowering anoja,[2] and betel[3] creepers grow there; and blossoming kiṁsuka creepers climb up a tree.

537 Kaṭeruhas,[4] vāsantis,[5] and yūthika jasmine[6] smelling sweet as honey; indigo plants, the great-flowered jasmine,[7] bhaṇḍi[8] plants, and padumuttara[9] plants stand in beauty.

Trumpet-flowers and sea-cotton[10] trees, and flowering kaṇikāras look like golden netting, brilliant as crests of flame.

Whatever flowers there are, which grow on land or in water, they are all to be seen there, and make that great stretch of water beautiful.

In that lotus-pond are many water-creatures: red-[fish], naḷapins,[11] siṅgu-fish, crocodiles, makaras,[12] and susus.

There is honey; liquorice plants, tāliṣa[13] shrubs, and panic seed[14] plants; fragrant unnaka[15] and bhaddamutta[16] grasses, dill[17] and lolupa.[18]

There are fragrant plants: tagara shrubs and tuṅgavaṇṭaka[19] flowers, padmaka, spikenard and kuṭṭha trees, jhāmaka[20] grass and sweet peas,[21]

The perfume-giving turmeric,[22] lemon-grass[23] and bdellium, palmyra, coraka,[24] kuṭṭha, camphor, and laurel.

And in that place are lions and tigers, purisālus[25] and elephants, antelopes, spotted deer, red deer, and sarabha deer;

[1] koraṇḍaka: *Skt.* kuraṇḍaka, *Carissa Carandas* (B, p. 17; C, p. 178).

[2] anoja: identification impossible.

[3] nāgavallika: *Skt.* nāgavallī/vallikā, *Piper betel* (B, p. 69).

[4] kaṭeruha: cf. p. 99, n. 12 above.

[5] vāsanti: *Skt.* vāsantī, *Goertnera racemosa* (B, p. 40).

[6] yūthika: *Skt.* yūthikā, *Jasminum auriculatum* (B, p. 48).

[7] sumanā: *Skt.* sumanā, possibly *Sarcostema viminialis*, or, M-W, *Rosa glandulifera.*

[8] bhaṇḍi: *Skt.* bhaṇḍī, *Rubia munjista.*

[9] padumuttara: *Skt.* padmottara, *Carthamus tinctorius* (B, p. 18).

[10] samuddakappāsi: *Skt.* karpāsa, *Gossypium herbaceum* (B, p. 40).

[11] naḷapin, siṅgu, susu: Comm. 'names of water-creatures'.

[12] makara: a kind of sea-monster, often mythical.

[13] tāliṣa: *Skt.* tālīśa, *Flacourtia cataphracta* (B, p. 38). (This plant and the following are said by Comm. to be types of perfume-giving plants.)

[14] piyaṅguka: *Skt.* priyaṅgu, *Panicum Italicum* (B, p. 66).

[15] unnaka: identification impossible.

[16] bhaddamutta: *Skt.* bhadramusta, *Cyperus rotundus* (B, p. 27).

[17] satapuppha: *Skt.* śatapuṣpa, *Anethum Sowa* (B, p. 6).

[18] lolupa: identification impossible.

[19] tuṅgavaṇṭaka (lit. having a long stalk): identification impossible.

[20] jhāmaka: identification impossible.

[21] hareṇuka: *Skt.* hareṇuka, possibly *Pisum sativum* (B, p. 70).

[22] haliddaka: haliddā: *Skt.* haridrā, *Curcuma longa* (B, p. 27).

[23] hirivera: *Skt.* hrīvera, *Andropogon schoenanthus* (B, p. 6).

[24] coraka: identification impossible.

[25] purisālu: Comm. suggests creatures with the face of a mare.

Jackals and dogs, small deer, and flying foxes the colour of reeds; yak oxen; the roaming antelope and the leaping antelope; monkeys and jhāpita and picu monkeys.

Kakkaṭas[1] and katamāyas,[2] bears and many wild oxen; rhinoceroses, 538
boars, and black mungooses are there in great numbers.

There are buffaloes, dogs, jackals, and apes on every side; iguanas, pacalākas,[3] spotted antelopes, and leopards;

Hares and vighāsādas,[4] lions, wolf-slayers, and octopods. There are the peacock, the bhassaras,[5] kukutthakas,[6]

Greek partridges, cocks and nāga [elephant/snake] birds crying out to one another; herons and cranes, gallinules and diṇḍibhas,[7] konch herons and vādikas,

The hawk, the red-backed bird, the pampaka[8] and jīvajīvaka pheasant, partridges and francolin partridges, kulāva[9] birds and paṭikuttakas;

Maddālakas[10] and cetakedus; the bald-headed bird,[11] partridge, and nāmaka; celāvakas and piṅgula owls,[12] godhakas and aṅgahetukas,

Indian cuckoos and high-flying saggas, owls and wild cocks. [The forest] is thronged with flocks of birds of many kinds, and echoes to their many and varied songs.

And in that place there are birds, dark-coloured and sweet-voiced, 539
singing out to one another happily, with their mates.

And in that place on the tops of setaccha trees there are birds, white birds with sweet songs, auspicious-eyed, born from an egg, with multi-coloured wings.

And in that place there are birds, white birds with sweet songs, with dark throats and crests, singing out to one another.

There are kukutthakas, crabs [?crab-birds], koṭṭha birds and cranes, kāḷāmeyyas and baḷīyakkhas, black geese, parrots, and saṁka birds.

[1] kakkaṭa: Comm. 'large deer/large animals'.

[2] katamāya: Comm. 'large deer/large animals'.

[3] pacalāka: *Skt.* pracalāka, chameleon, or snake, or other poisonous animal.

[4] vighāsāda (lit. one who eats remains of food): Comm. suggests a type of bird.

[5] bhassara (lit. shining, brilliant): Comm. 'white goose'.

[6] kukutthaka: *Skt.* kukkutaka, wild cock. Comm. 'kakuttha birds'.

[7] diṇḍibha, vādika: Comm. 'kinds of birds'.

[8] pampaka: presumably a kind of bird.

[9] kulāva paṭikuttaka: Comm. 'two kinds of birds'.

[10] maddālaka, cetakedu, celāvaka, godhaka, aṅgahetuka: presumably kinds of birds.

[11] bhanditittiranāmaka: possibly 'those called bald-headed partridges'.

[12] piṅgula: *Skt.* piṅgalā, a kind of owl.

[There are birds] in that place [the colour of] turmeric, red and white and black in great numbers; vāraṇa[1] and hiṅgurāja birds, black geese, parrots, and cuckoos;

Variegated ospreys, geese, āṭa birds[2] and parivadantika birds, pāka geese, atibalas,[3] gallinules, and jīvajīvaka pheasants,

Doves and sun-geese, ruddy geese keeping by the water, and vāraṇa birds with their beautiful notes, as they sing out in the morning and in the evening.

In that place are birds, many birds of all kinds of colours, singing out to one another happily, with their mates.

[1] vāraṇa: Comm. 'hatthiliṅga birds', possibly a kind of vulture.

[2] āṭa: Comm. 'a bird with a beak like a ladle'.

[3] atibala: ? (lit. 'very strong').

APPENDIX II

EMENDATIONS TO FAUSBØLL'S TEXT

ABBREVIATIONS

A	Alsdorf (see Bibliography)
Cp	*Cariyā-piṭaka* (see Bibliography)
Cpa	*Cariyā-piṭaka-aṭṭhakathā* (Commentary on Cp: see Bibliography)
F	Fausbøll's edition (see Bibliography)
H	Hewavitarane Bequest edition; i.e. readings reported in *Vds*, pp. 112–20, central column
PED	*Pali–English Dictionary*, ed. Rhys Davids and Stede, Pali Text Society, 1921–5
Vds	*Vesaturu-dā-sanne* (see Bibliography)
v.l.	*varia lectio*, i.e. variant reading reported by F

References are to page and line of Fausbøll's edition. Authority or justification for a change is given in brackets.

481. 29	cārupubbaṅgi] cārusabbaṅgi (A)
483. 1	nassantu] no santu (A)
483. 2	rāgo] rajo (Vds *and* H)
483. 4	khujjatecalākkhakākiṇṇe] khujjavelāmikākiṇṇe (Vds; *see also* PED *s.v.* velāmikā)
	sūdamāghatavaṇṇite] sūtamāgadhavaṇṇite (H)
483. 5	ughusite] ugghusite, *as separate word* (*follows from* A's *interpretation of* citraggaler *as instrumental plural*)
485. 1	Bodhisatassa] Bodhisattassa (*misprint*)
485. 17	jātamatte] jātamatto (*better grammar*)
485. 24	Mahāsattassa] Mahāsattaṃ (v.l. *and* Cpa; *see Introduction p.* xxxiv
485. 28	dāpsei] dāpesi (*misprint*)
486. 17	appoṭhesi] apphoṭesi (*misprint*)
486. 22	dadeyyaṃ kāyaṃ sāvetvā *is corrupt* (*the interpretation of* Cpa *is hopelessly far-fetched*) *and has been omitted in translation;* dadeyyaṃ *doubtless appears by diplography. Perhaps read* kāyaṃ sāmaṃ vadhitvāna (*cf.* v.l.)
488. 23	*read* ghaṇṭā *after* kaṇṇesu (v.l.)
489. 17–23	*should be in larger type—narrative mistakenly printed as commentary from* brāhmaṇā *on*

491. 14 mā naṃ daṇḍena satthena] mā naṃ satthena ghāteyya (A)
492. 7 asmā] asyā (A)
492. 11 *read* udakeso *as one word* (Vds *and* H)
492. 24 asmā] asyā (A)
493. 11 adakkhiṇaṃ] dakkhiṇaṃ (Vds)
493. 18 kāthento] kathento (*misprint*)
495. 19 saṃsayo] saṃsaye (A)
495. 23 abhumme kathaṃ bhaṇasi] abbhu me, kathan nu bhaṇasi (A)
495. 28 nijjālayitvāna] ujjālayitvāna (v.l. *and* Vds)
496. 4 gamissāmi] bhavissāmi (A)
496. 11 piyabhāṇino] piyabhāṇine (*cf. lines* 13 *and* 15)
496. 14, 18, 22, 26 kilante] kīḷante (A)
496. 25 dakhhisi] dakkhisi (*misprint*)
497. 4 kāmadaṃ] kāmada (A)
497. 22 *transpose verses* 96 *and* 97 (A)
497. 25 lomapadmakaṃ] loddapadmakaṃ (v.l. *and* Vds; *cf. Skt.* lodhra)
498. 13 paṭicchannayogena] paṭicchannayoggena (*better sense, and cf.* v.l.)
499. 5 nikhīṇapatto] nikkhīṇapatto (Vds *and* H)
500. 7–8 *verse* 115 *is obscure—corrupt?*
500. 24 Indassa gottassa] Indasagottassa (Vds *and* A)
502. 5 sabbā antepure bahu] antepure saddo ahu (Vds)
502. 13 heṭṭhāyittha] heṭhayittha (H)
502. 14 *At this point, after verse* 138, *should come the passage, wrongly printed in small type, from* 504. 1 (iti so . . .) *to* 504. 16 (. . . Satthā āha).
502. 15 te su mattā] te su-m-attā (A)
502. 26 atiyakkhā: *cf. Skt.* adhyakṣāḥ
503. 6 ajānīye] ājānīye (A)
503. 14 pītālaṃkārā pītavasanā] pītālaṃkāravasanā (A)
503. 15 aḷārapamukhā] aḷārapamhā (Vds; *cf. Skt.* arālapakṣma-)
susaññā] susoññā (F *suggests, following commentary*)
504. 17, 18 *delete* (*redundant after transposition of the preceding lines*)
506. 7 susaññā] susoññā (*cf.* 503, 15)
507. 1 ūpa nisevite] ūpanisevino *and delete colon* (A)
507. 7 tikkhaggā tippahārino] tikkhaggāni pahārino (H *and* A)
507. 11 dumagge suplavaṃgame] dumaggesu plavaṃgame (Vds, H *and* A)
507. 13 uttasayī] uttasase (H)
508. 1 muñjapabbajaṃ] muñjababbajaṃ (Vds *and* H)
508. 2 padahessāmi] panudahessāmi] (Vds, H, *and* A)
510. 4 sataphale] satapale (A)
510. 10 nivāse] nivāte (Vds)
510. 12 pallaṃkesu] pallañke su (Vds)
511. 9 āmanta kho taṃ *corrupt?*
512. 16 āgamiṃsu] agamiṃsu (A)
512. 26 assu pahato] ass'upahato (A)

514. 3 Arañjara] Ārañjara (v.l.; cf. 493.20)
514. 22 parikiriṃsu] parikariṃsu (Vds *and* H)
515. 7 ārogo] arogo (A)
515. 27 sammā] samma (A)
516. 2 *delete full stop*
517. 5, 9 rajjassa-m-anusāsituṃ] rajjaṃ samanusāsituṃ (A)
517. 12 hi secayuṃ] 'bhisecayuṃ (Vds, H *and* A)
517. 16 hiṃseyyuṃ bahuke jane] hiṃseyya bahuko jano (v.l. *and* Vds)
518. 6 c'acchasi] vacchasi (A)
518. 26 girividuggānaṃ] girividuggāni (Vds, H *and* A)
519. 19 sakalanagaraṃ] sakanagaraṃ (A)
519. 28 pavisi tvātaṃ] pavisitvā taṃ (*misprint*)
520. 4 caṅkammakoṭiyaṃ] caṅkamakoṭiyaṃ (*misprint*)
521. 21 ahu vāsī] ahuvāsi (A)
521. 22 tassāpi] tassāsi (A)
521. 23 tattha gatā] titthagatā (A)
521. 26, 28, 522.5 sati] satiṃ (A)
522. 1, 9 dahariyaṃ sati] dahariyā satī (A)
522. 4 jiṇṇa] jiṇṇassa (A)
522. 6 ye] yā (A)
522. 10 daḍḍhaṃ] daṭṭhaṃ (Vds *and* H)
524. 2 ayuddho] ayuddhe (A)
524. 2, 3 āgantvā] agantvā (Vds *and* A)
525. 2 katvā] vatvā (v.l., Vds *and* H)
525. 25 brāmaṇiyā] brāhmaṇiyā (*misprint*)
526. 8–9 so sunakhehi . . . *should be in larger type—narrative printed as commentary*
526. 15 mahārajaṃ] mahārājaṃ (*misprint*)
526. 21 mahārāyaṃ] mahārājaṃ (*misprint*)
526. 29 tathūpamaṃ] saṃtānaṃ (A)
527. 17 dummedho] dummedha (v.l. *and* Vds)
527. 20 pāssati] passati (A)
528. 24, 529. 4, 530. 27, 532. 3, 533. 29, 533. 32 *read* camasañ jaṭaṃ (PED, *s.v.* masa)
528. 29 sampavedhenti] sampavedhanti (Vds *and* H)
529. 21 padarāni] badarāni (Vds, H *and* PED)
529. 23 madhumadhukā] madhuṃ madhukā (A)
529. 33 dhajaggān'eva] dhajaggānīva (A)
530. 3 uddhālakā] uddālakā (Vds, H *and* PED)
530. 9 nuñjubhāṇikā] mañjubhāṇikā (H *and* A)
530. 15 macchakacchapavyāvidhā] macchakacchapā vyāviddhā (A; Vds *and* H *read* macchakacchapavyāviddhā)
530. 20 nānāvaṇṇabahū] nānāvaṇṇā bahū (*better grammar*)
530. 22 no] te (Vds *and* A)
531. 33 hi] pi (v.l., Vds *and* H)
532. 16, 23 appam eva] appa-m-eva (A)
532. 29 tiṇḍukāni] tindukāni (Vds, H, *and* PED)
533. 8 mañye] mañña (*misprint*)

533. 15 bhotā] bhoto (A)
534. 2 sampavedhenti] sampavedhanti (*see* 528. 29)
534. 29 setasogandhigehi] setasogandhiyehi (Vds *and* PED)
535. 11 setavārisā] setapārisā (Vds *and* H)
535. 15 mahānāmā] kaṇaverā (Vds *and* H)
536. 11 kaṭerukkhehi] kaṭerukehi (Vds *and* H)
536. 14 kakkaru] kakkāru (Vds *and* H)
536. 34 korandakā] koraṇḍakā (Vds *and* H)
538. 6 romā] morā (v.l., Vds *and* H)
538. 9 vyaghīnasā] vyagghīnasā (Vds *and* H)
538. 14 nikujjitan] nikūjitan (Vds)
539. 27 nivāro] nīvāro (Vds *and* H)
539. 28 va] ca (Vds *and* H)
542. 13 appam eva] appa-m-eva (A)
542. 16 kusulañ] kusalañ (*misprint*)
542. 21 imam] idaṃ (A)
543. 18 *delete* (A)
544. 29 jino] jīno (Vds *and* H)
545. 4 muñjuke] mañjuke (*misprint*)
545. 16 ḍalhaṃ] daḷhaṃ (*misprint*)
547. 21 sukhavacchite] sukhavajjite (A)
548. 29 valīnaṃ] valinaṃ (A)
548. 30 brahā kharo] brahākaro (Vds *and* A)
549. 4 asmā] asmā ha (A)
551. 19 arabbha] ārabbha (*misprint*)
551. 27 *should be in larger type—prose printed as verse*
551. 29 ne] no (A)
552. 2 santāsunehi] santā sunehi (Vds *and* H *read* sūṇehi; *cf.* 555. 17, *below*)
552. 30 *delete* taṃ (A)
553. 12 sakāmatā] sakā mātā (*better sense*)
553. 14 amhā ti] amhāsi (A)
555. 13 sambhati] sumbhati (*misprint*)
555. 17 sutā] sunā (A; Vds *and* H *read* sūṇā)
556. 8 sīhavyagghadīpivesena] sīhavyagghadīpivese (A)
556. 19 Jātikumār'] Jālikumār' (*misprint*)
557. 12 bhuñjeyyuṃ] bhuñjeyyu (A)
558. 31 patthā] panthā (Vds *and* H)
559. 20 chakalīva migī] chakalimva migiṃ (Vds, H *and* F)
559. 26 me vicinanti *is corrupt*; A *suggests* m'eko *followed by a trisyllabic verb. The general sense is clear. Perhaps read* ucchañg' eko vivattati?
560. 34 ayyaputtā] ayyaputta (*misprint, corrected by* F, *p.* 599)
560. 35 īrine] iriṇe (Vds *and* H)
562. 3–9 Maddi tvaṃ . . . *to end of paragraph should be in larger type—narrative printed as commentary.*
562. 13 *delete* me (A)
563. 4 tuyhaṃ kāmāhi] tumhaṃ kāmā hi (A)

563. 10 puttā ti] puttāni (Vds, H *and* A)
564. 22 cittapekkhanā] cittapekhuṇā (Vds *and* H *read* citrapekkhuṇā)
565. 31 paridevitvā] paridhāvitvā (*better sense*)
565. 32 puna-d-ev'] puna-d-eva (A)
566. 8 patitā] papatā (v.l., *explained by Professor von Hinüber as reduplicated aorist form*)
566. 29 Saṃ] Taṃ (*misprint*)
567. 6 na kātum] n'akkhātum (Vds; *this is also read by the commentator in* F)
568. 16–19 *these lines of prose belong between verses* 610 *and* 611
568. 19 *delete* iti Maddīti (*rendered redundant by previous emendation*)
569. 5, 10 appam eva] appa-m-eva (A)
569. 31 asajjetvā] asajjitvā (v.l. *makes better sense*)
570. 15–17 ambho . . . *to end of paragraph should be in larger type—narrative printed as commentary*
572. 5 sammataassame] sammatha assame (A, *following* F's *suggestion in note*)
572. 6 sajātā] sujātā (Vds *and* H)
572. 25 *delete first* ca (A)
572. 29 yo] so (Vds *and* H)
575. 2 *corrupt: probable meaning in translation; punctuate* na saddahe
575. 18 *punctuate* assatarīratham (A)
575. 29 *punctuate* assatarīratho (*follows from previous correction*)
575. 28 bāhunā chaḍḍento] bāhaṃ oḍḍento (H; *cf.* v.l.)
576. 2 nu] tu (A)
576. 6 h'eva] hīva (A)
576. 28 maṃ] me (A)
576. 29 daṇḍena] dabbena (Vds; *cf.* F, *p.* 577, *note* 1)
577. 30 bhaṇḍe] bhaṇḍena (Vds, H *and* A)
578. 3 kuṇḍale ghusite māle] kuṇḍalaghusite mālī (A)
578. 5 ārogā] arogā (*cf. line* 13)
578. 7, 15 appam eva] appa-m-eva (A)
578. 13 me] te (A)
578. 17–20 *verses* 681 *and* 682 *should come after verse* 684 (A)
578. 23 *punctuate* patanū kesā (A)
578. 35 putte sineho] puttasineho (v.l., Vds *and* A)
579. 4 adosakaṃ] adūsakaṃ (Vds)
579. 12 devo] deva (A)
579. 20 nīlavaṇṇadharā] nīlavatthadharā (Vds); *and punctuate to eliminate spaces before* neke (< aneke) (A)
579. 21 aññe lohitatuṇhīsā] aneke lohit'uṇhīsā *and punctuate* suddhāneke (A)
579. 23 Gandharo] gandhadharo (Vds *and* H)
579. 26 *second half of line* (disā . . .) *corrupt—diplography from previous line* (A)
580. 25 naṭanaṭṭakagāyanā] naṭanaccakagāyakā (Vds)
580. 28 dhamantu vadataṃ] dhammantu vadantaṃ (A; H *reads* dhammantu vadataṃ)

583. 18–20 *read* gaccheyyāsi, atha thokaṃ kālaṃ vītināmetvā Jālī ca Kaṇhājinā ca pacchato āgacchantū' ti vatvā (*i.e. mainly follow the* v.l.; *Sañjaya can hardly address his grandchildren in the third person*)
583. 24 seniyo] seṇiyo (*misprint?*)
584. 4, 586. 7 husā] nusā (< *Skt.* snuṣā)
584. 13 appam eva] appa-m-eva (A)
584. 17 kasirā hi jīvikā] kasirājīvikā; *and delete full stop* (A)
586. 18–26 sā kira mahantena . . . *should be in larger type—narrative printed as commentary*
586. 25 sakalaassamapadaṃ] sakalaṃ assamapadaṃ (*parallel passage in* Cpa)
587. 7 samapajjatha] samagacchatha (Vds *and* H; *cf.* v.l.)
587. 9 *delete comma and substitute full stop* (A)
587. 10 tassa] taṃ; *and delete full stop*; verse 746 *starts here* (A) bheravā] bherave (Vds *and* H)
589. 23 *punctuate* kāmā hi (A)
589. 24 *delete second* taṃ (A)
589. 26 *repeats* line 3 *above* (verse 753), *not very appropriately; should probably be deleted*
590. 7 khomañ] hemañ (v.l., *apparently glossed by commentary*)
590. 19 cittapattā pati] cittapatattinī (<*Skt.*-patatriṇī; *something needed to save grammar and metre*)
590. 20 nigrodhapattabimboṭṭhī] nigrodhapakkabimboṭṭhī (Vds, H *and commentator in* F)
593. 14–15 vaṭṭadhanaṃ] vaṭṭhadhanaṃ; *and move opening quotation marks to follow the word*

We have omitted nothing printed by F in square brackets. A has shown that words bracketed for metrical reasons, as constituting a fifth *pāda*, are genuine. He suspects vv. 58–9 (p. 493, lines 8–12) and vv. 609–10 (p. 568, lines 3–4 and 7–10) of being interpolated; but the interpolations would be ancient, perhaps contemporary with the prose stratum.

BIBLIOGRAPHY

This is a bibliography of material referred to in the Introduction. For fuller bibliographies see

Lamotte, É., *La Somme du Grand Véhicule d'Asanga*, Louvain, 1938, p. 43*.

Lamotte, É., *Le Traité de la Grande Vertu de Sagesse de Nāgārjuna*, vol. ii, Louvain, 1949, pp. 713–14.

A. VERSIONS OF THE *VESSANTARA JĀTAKA*

(i) VERSIONS WHOLLY OR PARTLY IN PĀLI

Cariyā-piṭaka. VJ on pp. 78–81 in *Buddhavaṃsa and Cariyāpiṭaka*, ed. R. Morris, Pali Text Society, London, 1882.

Cariyā-piṭaka-aṭṭhakathā. VJ on pp. 74–102 of *Paramatthadīpanī*, ed. D. L. Barua, Pali Text Society, London, 1939.

Vesaturu-dā-sanne, ed. D. E. Hettiaratchi, Colombo, 1950.

Vessantara Jātaka, pp. 479–596 in *Jātaka*, vol. vi, ed. V. Fausbøll, London, 1896, reprinted Pali Text Society, London, 1964.

Vessantara Jātaka, trans. W. H. D. Rouse. pp. 246–305 in *The Jātaka*, vol. vi, trans. E. B. Cowell and W. H. D. Rouse, Cambridge, 1907.

(ii) VERSIONS IN OTHER LANGUAGES

Burmese

Goss, L. Allan, *The Story of We-than-da-ya*, Rangoon, 1886.

White, O., *A Literal Translation of the Text Book Committee's Edition of Wethandaya*, Rangoon, 1896.

Chinese

Chavannes, É., *Cinq cent contes et apologues*, 4 vols., Paris. *VJ* in vol. iii, 1911, pp. 362–95.

Khotanese

Dresden, Mark J., *The Jātakastava or 'Praise of the Buddha's Former Births'*, *Transactions of the American Philosophical Society*, N.S. vol. 45, part 5, Philadelphia, 1955. *VJ* on pp. 441, 444, 452.

Sanskrit

Ārya Śūra, *Jātakamālā*, ed. H. Kern, Harvard Oriental Series, Cambridge, Mass., 1891. *VJ* on pp. 51–67.

Ārya Śura, *Jātakamālā*, trans. J. S. Speyer, *Sacred Books of the Buddhists*, vol. i, London, 1895. *VJ* on pp. 71–93.

Kṣemendra, *Avadānakalpalatā*, ed. S. C. Das and H. M. Vidyābhūshaṇa, Calcutta, 1888. *VJ* in vol. i, pp. 646–61.

Somadeva, *Kathāsaritsāgara*, ed. Durgāprasād and K. P. Parab, 3rd edn., Bombay, 1915. *VJ* (story of Tārāvaloka) on pp. 535–7.

Somadeva, *The Ocean of Story* [i.e. *Kathāsaritsāgara*], trans. C. H. Tawney, London, 1924–8. *VJ* (Tārāvaloka) in vol. viii, pp. 125–31.

Sinhalese

Da Silvā, Jōn, (John De Silva), *Vessantara Jātaka Nāṭyaya*, Colombo, n.d. (originally published *c.* 1920?).

Vessantara Jātaka Kāvyaya, ed. R. Vijayatilaka, Colombo, 1947.

Sogdian

Benveniste, É., *Vessantara Jātaka*, Paris, 1946.

Tibetan

Bacot, J., 'Drimedkundan. Une Version Tibétaine dialoguée du *Vessantara Jātaka*', *Journal asiatique*, XIe série, Paris, 1914, pp. 221–305.

Von Schiefner, F. A., (trans.), *Tibetan Tales*, 'done into English' by W. R. S. Ralston, London, 1882. *VJ* on pp. 257–72, trans. from *Kahgyur*, IV, folia 192–200.

For another version in Tibetan see Kṣemendra above.

Tocharian

Sieg, E., and Siegling, W., *Tocharische Sprachreste*, vol. i, Berlin and Leipzig, 1921. *VJ* on p. 41, No. 70, and p. 197, No. 356.

Sieg, E., *Uebersetzungen aus dem Tocharischen*, *Abhandlungen der Deutschen Akademie der Wissenschaften zu Berlin, Klasse für Sprachen, Literatur und Kunst*, No. 1, 1951. *VJ* on pp. 43–4.

B. MODERN WORKS

Alsdorf, L., 'Bemerkungen zum Vessantara-Jātaka', *Wiener Zeitschrift für die Kunde Süd- und Ostasiens*, vol. i, 1957, pp. 1–70.

Chavannes, E., 'Voyage de Song Yun dans l'Udyāna et la Gandhāra (518–522 p.C.)', *Bulletin de l'École française d'extrême orient*, vol. iii, 1903, pp. 379–429. *VJ* on pp. 413–14 and 419–20.

Coomaraswamy, A. K., *Mediaeval Sinhalese Art*, 2nd. edn., New York, 1956.

Foucher, A., 'Notes sur la géographie ancienne du Gandhâra', *Bulletin de l'École française d'extrême orient*, vol. i, 1901, pp. 322–69. *VJ* on pp. 350–9.

Godakumbura, C. E., *Medawala Vihara Frescoes*, Archaeological Department, Colombo, n.d. (1964?).

Karpelès, S., 'Voyage au Laos', *Bulletin de l'École française d'extrême orient*, vol. xxxi, 1931, pp. 331–4. *VJ* on p. 332.

Keith, A. B., *History of Sanskrit Literature*, London, 1920.

Leclère, A., *Cambodge, Fêtes Civiles et Religieuses*, Paris, 1947. *VJ* on pp. 415–18.

Sarachchandra, E. R., *The Folk Drama of Ceylon*, 2nd edn., Colombo, 1966.

Spiro, Melford E., *Buddhism and Society*, New York and Evanston, 1970.

Tambiah, S. J., 'The Ideology of Merit and the Social Correlates of Buddhism in a Thai Village', pp. 41–121 in E. R. Leach (ed.), *Dialectic in Practical Religion*, *Cambridge Papers in Social Anthropology*, No. 5, Cambridge, 1968. *VJ* on pp. 77–82.